W9-CAL-402

ENVIRONMENTAL DISASTERS

The San Francisco Earthquake

Richard Worth

☑®

Facts On File, Inc.

The San Francisco Earthquake

Copyright © 2005 by Facts On File, Inc.

Facts On File, Inc.
132 West 31st Street
New York NY 10001

Library of Congress Cataloging-in-Publication Data

Worth, Richard.
  The San Franciso earthquake / Richard Worth.
    p. cm. — (Environmental disasters)
  Includes bibliographical references and index.
  ISBN 0-8160-5756-7 (hc: acid-free paper)
    1. San Francisco Earthquake, Calif., 1906—Juvenile literature.
  2. Earthquakes—California—San Francisco—History—20th century—Juvenile literature. I. Title. II. Environmental disasters (Facts On File)
QE536.2.U5W67 2005
363.34'95'0979461—dc22   2004059148

A Creative Media Applications, Inc. Production
Writer: Richard Worth
Design and Production: Alan Barnett, Inc.
Editor: Matt Levine
Copy Editor: Laurie Lieb
Proofreader: Laurie Lieb
Indexer: Nara Wood
Associated Press Photo Researcher: Yvette Reyes
Consultant: Thomas A. Birkland, Nelson A. Rockefeller College of Public Affairs
    and Policy, University at Albany, State University of New York
Graph by Rolin Graphics

Contents

Preface

This book is about the tragic San Francisco earthquake of 1906. On April 18, 1906, the quake struck California's Bay Area, and with its resulting fires left over 500 people dead and more than $500 million worth of damage. The map on the next page shows the San Andreas fault, along which the quake took place, and its location in relation to the city of San Francisco.

Almost everyone is curious about such catastrophic events. An interest in these disasters, as shown by the decision to read this book, is the first step on a fascinating path toward learning how disasters occur, why they are feared, and what can be done to prevent them from hurting people, as well as their homes and businesses.

The word *disaster* comes from the Latin for "bad star." Thousands of years ago, people believed that certain alignments of the stars influenced events on Earth, including natural disasters. Today, natural disasters are sometimes called "acts of God" because no human made them happen. Scientists now know that earthquakes, hurricanes, and volcanic eruptions occur because of natural processes that the scientists can explain much better than they could even a few years ago.

An event is usually called a disaster only if it hurts people. For example, an earthquake occurred along Alaska's Denali fault in 2002. Although this earthquake had a magnitude of 7.9, it killed no one and did little serious damage. But a "smaller" earthquake—with a magnitude below 7.0—in Kobe, Japan, in 1995 did billions of dollars in damage and killed about 5,100 people. This quake was considered a disaster.

A disaster may also damage animals and the environment. The *Exxon Valdez* oil spill in Alaska is considered a disaster because it injured and killed hundreds of birds, otters, deer, and other animals. The spill also killed thousands of fish—which

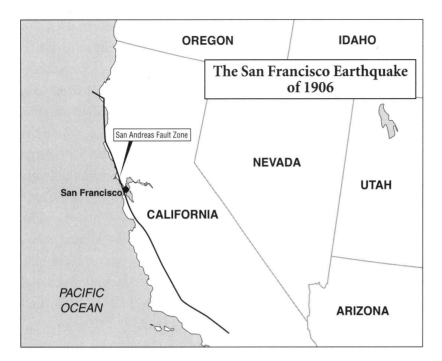

The San Francisco Earthquake of 1906

San Andreas Fault Zone

San Francisco

PACIFIC OCEAN

OREGON

IDAHO

NEVADA

UTAH

CALIFORNIA

ARIZONA

many Alaskan fishers rely on to earn their livelihoods—and polluted the places where the fish spawn.

Disasters are also more likely to happen when people make decisions that leave them *vulnerable* to catastrophe. For example, a beachside community is more vulnerable to a hurricane than a community that is inland from the ocean. When people choose where to live, they are also choosing what sort of natural disasters they may experience in the future; they are choosing the sort of risks they are willing to take. People who live on beaches in Florida know that hurricanes may damage or destroy their houses; people who live in certain areas of California know that earthquakes may strike at any time.

The things that people do to make themselves safer from less dangerous natural events, like heavy rains, sometimes actually make the people more vulnerable to bigger disasters. For example, when a dam is built on a river to protect people downstream from floods, the dam may prevent small floods that would otherwise happen once every 25 years. But when a really big storm occurs—the kind that comes once every 100 years—the dam may not be able to hold back the water. Then a surge of water that is even bigger than it would have been without the dam will come rushing down the river and completely destroy all the buildings in the area.

At first, it may seem easy to blame human disasters, like the *Exxon Valdez* spill, on one or a few people. Some observers blame the spill on the captain, who was responsible for the ship. But perhaps the spill was another crewmember's fault. Maybe the blame should fall on Exxon, because that corporation owned the ship. Or maybe all Americans are to blame, because the United States uses a lot of oil for heating houses and driving cars. Finding the "right people" to blame can be difficult. Is it anyone's fault that people suffer from natural disasters? Natural disasters at first appear to be merely unfortunate "acts of God."

This book and the other books in this series will demonstrate that mistakes people made before a disaster often made the disaster worse than it should have been. But they will also show how many people work to lessen the damage caused by disasters. Firefighters, sailors, and police officers, for example, work very hard right after disasters to rescue people, limit additional damage, and help people get back to their normal lives. Behind the scenes are engineers, architects, legislators, scientists, and other citizens working to design new buildings, make new rules about how and where to build buildings, and enforce those rules so that fewer people will have to risk their lives due to disasters.

The books in this series will show what can be done to reduce the chances that people and communities will suffer from natural and human disasters. Everyone has a role to play in making communities safer. The books in this series can show readers how to become part of a growing movement of citizens and experts that can help everyone make good decisions about disasters.

Please note: All metric conversions in this book are approximate.

Introduction

Natural disasters are events that occur spontaneously in nature and leave damage and destruction in their wake. People may lose their homes, their businesses, or even their lives. The environment may also suffer damage. Often, people can rebuild what has been taken from them by a natural disaster, but many can never forget what happened to them or regain what they lost.

Earthquakes are among the most frightening natural disasters facing human beings. They occur all over the world every day—but only the largest earthquakes cause loss of human life and billions of dollars in damages. Before modern science, different cultures had their own ways of explaining quakes. Ancient peoples in India believed that the earth was held up by four elephants standing on the back of a turtle balanced on top of a cobra. If any of those animals moved, the earth would shake and tremble. West African legend told of a giant that carried the earth on his head. When he turned his head to face a different direction, the earth moved with him.

An earthquake is a sudden movement inside Earth caused by an abrupt release of energy that has accumulated over a long period of time. Underneath Earth's surface are large plates of rock that constantly shift around each other. Sometimes, these plates become locked together and strain against each other. The energy from that resistance becomes so great that when the plates finally break free from each other, they cause a burst of movement inside Earth.

The study of earthquakes is a relatively new science. Before the 1900s, there were few records of these natural phenomena. Today, scientists try to monitor and predict them. They study where and when earthquakes have occurred in the past in order to understand where they might occur in the future. Early prediction of earthquakes is very important to society. As the population of the

Enrico Caruso was a well-known opera singer visiting San Francisco at the time of the earthquake. He famously sang for crowds following the earthquake in an effort to provide comfort and hope for the days ahead. (Photo courtesy of Associated Press)

United States continues to grow, cities will expand. Some cities will develop in areas where another earthquake is bound to occur.

In the aftermath of a large earthquake, buildings are destroyed, water supplies may become contaminated, power shuts down, and roads and bridges collapse. The priority of researchers examining earthquakes is to be able to warn people in advance of a large quake so that they will have enough time to put safety precautions and evacuation plans into action.

There have been several severe and deadly earthquakes around the world in the recent past. On January 26, 2001, a massive earthquake in India killed over 20,000 people and severely damaged roads and bridges. The largest earthquake in southeastern Iran in 2,000 years destroyed 85 percent of the region's buildings and infrastructure in December 2003. Over 30,000 people were killed. In North America, an earthquake rocked the California city of Northridge, near Los Angeles, on January 17, 1994. The Northridge earthquake was the first in North America to strike directly underneath an urban area since an earthquake in Long Beach, California, in 1933. During the Northridge quake, scientists tracked the strongest ground motions ever instrumentally recorded. Office and apartment buildings were destroyed. Homes were damaged. Sections of the freeway broke apart. Although only 57 people died from the quake, it was the costliest natural disaster in U.S. history.

Seventy percent of the world's earthquakes occur along the Pacific Rim, the countries and landmasses surrounding the Pacific Ocean. In North America, this means the majority of severe earthquakes are experienced in California. However, the most widely felt earthquakes in the recorded history of North America occurred in Missouri in 1811 and 1812. Although the trembling of the ground was felt as far away as Massachusetts and Colorado, these earthquakes occurred in rural areas and did little damage.

The same was not true of the San Francisco earthquake of 1906. That earthquake destroyed the young city of San Francisco, killed hundreds of people, and left thousands more lost and homeless.

The study of the San Francisco earthquake, the destruction that it caused, and its aftermath paved the way for new building techniques, more advanced firefighting methods, and better disaster response methods. *The San Francisco Earthquake* describes the earthquake, how and why it caused such damage, how it affected individuals, and how San Francisco was able to rebuild itself into a thriving city once again. The book concludes with a time line, a chronology of earthquakes, a glossary, and a list of sources (books and web sites) for further information.

Please note: Glossary words are in italics the first time that they appear in the text. Other words defined in the text may also be in italics.

CHAPTER 1

Understanding Earthquakes

Late in the 19th century, geologist Andrew Lawson discovered that San Francisco and the surrounding areas lie along a great *fault,* or crack in Earth's surface. Lawson called this crack the *San Andreas fault,* after nearby San Andreas Lake. Fault lines open up where large sections of Earth's crust—called plates—come together. According to the theory of *plate tectonics,* these crustal *plates* are constantly in motion, riding on a layer of very hot, soft rock. As they come in contact, one plate may dip underneath another, or two plates may slide by each other.

The major earthquakes along the San Andreas fault can be detected in the changes of earth seen in this photograph. Doug Yule, associate professor of geology at California State University, Northridge, examines the different soil mixtures of light-colored rock and gravel and dark-colored peat to piece together the changes seismic activity brings. (Photo courtesy of Associated Press)

Among these large plates are the North American plate and the Pacific plate. These plates are slowly and continually sliding to the right of each other along the San Andreas fault. The San Andreas fault runs for approximately 600 miles (965 km) along the floor of the Pacific Ocean northwest of California, down the coastal region of the state, and all the way to its southeastern corner. Scientists believe that as the Pacific plate and the North American plate move past each other in different directions at a rate of about 1 to 1.5 inches (2.5 to 3.8 cm) per year, rocks at the ends of each plate become locked together. As the plates continue to move, tension builds up in these rocks. Once the tension becomes too great, the rocks break apart with a violent motion, slipping up, down, or sideways in opposite directions. The result is a powerful earthquake like the one that occurred in 1906.

Earthquake Destruction

In 1906 the San Francisco earthquake began along the Pacific Ocean seafloor and rapidly reached shore at a speed of 7,000 miles (11,260 km) an hour. An earthquake begins many miles beneath the surface, at an area known as the *focus* or hypocenter. Along the surface, the point directly above the *hypocenter* is called the *epicenter* of the earthquake. The epicenter of the 1906 earthquake was located at sea, off the coast of San Francisco. Earthquakes send out massive vibrations known as *seismic waves*. These move rapidly through rocks, pushing them against each other and driving them apart.

From the epicenter, seismic waves travel outward. Surface waves travel along the surface of the ground. Body waves travel underground, through Earth, causing the most destruction. The fastest-moving body waves, known as *primary* or *P waves*, move at 2.5 to 4.3 miles (4 to 7 km) per second through the earth until they eventually reach the surface. Other body waves, called *secondary* or *S waves*, move more slowly, at about half the speed of the P waves. The secondary body waves move the ground horizontally and vertically, making roads move up and down, and shaking buildings, causing them to collapse. Many buildings collapsed during the great San Francisco earthquake of 1906, leaving the city devastated.

Recording Earthquakes

During the last quarter of the 19th century, geology professor John Milne developed the modern *seismograph* to measure the size of earthquakes. Although Milne was born in Great Britain, he spent part of his career studying earthquakes in Tokyo, Japan—an area where quakes occur regularly. The seismograph developed by Milne used a frame that moved back and forth as an earthquake occurred. From the frame, Milne hung a heavy weight that tended to remain steadier during the shaking of an earthquake. A roll of

This picture shows an early model of the seismograph, the machine John Milne invented to study the size of earthquakes. (Photo courtesy of Anne Domdey/ CORBIS)

A German Seismogram

This seismogram shows the ground movement in Göttingen, Germany, as a result of the 1906 San Francisco earthquake, which struck 9,100 miles (14,600 km) away. The seismogram—an example of how far away from their source seismic waves can be detected—was recorded over the span of about 26 minutes. The small up-and-down lines show the effect of the P waves, while the larger lines show the arrival of the S waves. The seismogram ends with the arrival of surface waves, which sent the seismograph off the scale.

paper moved by a revolving drum scrolled by under the weight. A writing instrument attached to the end of the weight recorded information on the paper as it moved past. When a powerful quake occurred, the seismograph recorded lines that zigged and zagged wildly along the roll of paper.

Milne's invention was used in earthquake recording centers throughout the world. When the San Francisco earthquake struck, seismographs in recording centers as far away as Moscow, Russia, and Cape Town, South Africa, picked up the waves sent out by the quake.

As seismographs became more sophisticated, they used electric devices and computers to increase their sensitivity to seismic waves and magnify the size of the pictures that the waves created on them. As a result, scientists improved their ability to detect even minor earthquakes. Currently, the National Earthquake Information Center (NEIC), maintained by the U.S. government in Golden, Colorado, constantly receives information from *seismograms*. A seismogram is a graph of an earthquake that has been created by a seismograph. The sidebar "A German Seismogram" to the left further examines one of these graphs. Seismograms are sent to the NEIC from earthquake stations around the world. With this information, the center can monitor the location of earthquakes and plate movements, as well as the size and strength of quakes. The NEIC is part of the U.S. Geological Survey (USGS). Located in Reston, Virginia, the USGS monitors Earth's structures and provides information about natural resources, as well as natural disasters such as earthquakes and volcanic eruptions.

Measuring Earthquakes

Seismologists, scientists who study earthquakes, use various methods of measuring the strength of a quake. In 1902 an Italian scientist, Giuseppe Mercalli, developed the *Mercalli scale,* later called the *modified Mercalli intensity scale.* The scale records the amount of damage caused by a quake, using a grade from I to XII. This scale is shown in detail in the "Modified Mercalli Scale" sidebar on page 6.

During the 1930s, Charles F. Richter, an American seismologist, developed another scale. Called the *Richter scale,* it measures the amount of energy produced by an earthquake. In this scale, each number represents a release of energy about ten times greater than

Dr. Charles F. Richter developed the first magnitude scale, known as the Richter scale, for earthquakes. Scientists today are still trying to fulfill Richter's vision of earthquakes as something that can be predicted and guarded against. (Photo courtesy of Bettmann/CORBIS)

The Modified Mercalli Scale

I.   Only a few people feel the earthquake

II. Only people on upper floors of buildings feel the earthquake

III. Vibration is felt that is similar to that from a passing truck; automobiles may move back and forth

IV. Many people indoors feel the earthquake; doors, windows, and dishes move

V.   Buildings and trees tremble; most people feel the earthquake; some dishes are broken

VI. Everyone feels the earthquake; plaster is damaged

VII. Buildings suffer damage; it is difficult for people to stand

VIII. Heavy damage is done to weak buildings; chimneys and factory stacks are overturned

IX. Pipes crack and buildings collapse

X–XI. Many buildings are destroyed

XII. All buildings are destroyed

the preceding number. The Richter scale runs from 0 to 9, although some of the most massive recorded quakes have been measured at over 9. Large, destructive earthquakes register 7 or above on the Richter scale. Another measuring system, called the *moment magnitude scale,* measures large earthquakes using devices far more sensitive than those used by Richter. The sidebar "Earthquake Magnitudes along the San Andreas Fault" on page 8 gives examples of some Richter magnitudes from California quakes.

Powerful Earthquakes

Powerful quakes occur not only along the San Andreas fault, but also in other parts of the world where plates come in contact with each other. Earthquakes can also occur along faults within a single plate. An example is the series of three earthquakes that occurred in New Madrid, Missouri, in 1811 and 1812. Although the magnitudes of the quakes were not recorded at the time, scientists estimate that they may have reached 8 on the Richter scale.

Massive earthquakes have also occurred in other parts of the world. Many quakes occur around the rim of the Pacific Ocean, where crustal plates push up against each other. In 1923, for example, a giant earthquake outside of Tokyo killed 143,000 people. In 1960 an earthquake that measured 9.5 on the Richter scale destroyed large areas of Chile. This earthquake also unleashed a giant *tsunami*. This is a Japanese word meaning "harbor wave." Tsunamis result

The 1960 earthquake in Chile destroyed the towns of Valdivia and Puerto Montt because of their proximity to the center of the quake. Although the quake caused millions of dollars' worth of property damage, many people escaped with their lives because foreshocks 30 minutes earlier had warned them to leave their homes and take to the streets. (Photo courtesy of Associated Press)

Earthquake Magnitudes along the San Andreas Fault

Location	Richter Magnitude
Santa Barbara, 1812	7.0
Wrightwood, 1812	7.0
San Francisco, 1838	7.0
Fort Tejon, 1857	8.3
San Francisco, 1906	*8.3*
San Jacinto, 1918	6.9
Loma Prieta (San Francisco), 1989	7.1
Northridge (Los Angeles), 1994	6.7

from shock waves created by earthquakes. As they move across the ocean toward land, tsunamis can reach huge heights. The tsunami that hit Chile in 1960 reached 50 feet (15.2 m). Over 5,500 people are thought to have died in Chile from the earthquake and resulting tsunami. The tsunami reached 35 feet (11 m) as far away as Hawaii, where over 60 people died when the wave hit the shore.

Another massive earthquake struck in the Andes Mountains of Peru in 1970, killing 66,000 people in the towns of Yungay and Ranrahirca. These towns were buried under a landslide. Landslides caused by earthquakes not only kill many people in their path, but also cause environmental damage. Trees and forests are uprooted, farms are destroyed, and rivers are polluted by debris. An even more devastating quake struck the city of Tangshan in China in 1976, with an official death toll of 255,000. More recently, an earthquake measuring 7.9 on the Richter scale destroyed a large area of northwestern India in 2001, killing almost 20,000 people and destroying the homes of 1 million Indian farmers. On December 26, 2003, the city of Bam in southern Iran was hit by a gigantic quake that killed over 30,000 people. This quake measured 6.6 on the Richter scale.

The History of San Francisco Earthquakes

In certain geographical locations, such as Iran, Japan, the South American coast, and California, earthquakes have struck repeatedly over the centuries. One California earthquake was recorded during the summer of 1769, when an expedition of Spanish soldiers traveled up the coast. The soldiers' journey had begun in Mexico, which had been conquered by the Spanish more than two centuries earlier with the defeat of the powerful empire of the Aztecs. Since that time, the Spanish had established outposts in Lower, or Baja, California. The Spanish government then decided to occupy Upper, or Alta, California to prevent British and Russian traders in Canada from gaining a foothold in the area.

The expedition left Mexico in January 1769, under the command of Don Gaspar de Portolá, the governor of Baja. On July 1, Portola reached San Diego, where he established a military post, or *presidio*. Portola then headed northward. Along with the Spanish soldiers went Father Juan Crespi, who kept a journal of the expedition. About two weeks' journey north of San Diego, Crespi wrote that "we experienced here a horrifying earthquake, which was repeated four times during the day." This quake is believed to be the first recorded by Europeans in California.

The Spanish established a settlement at San Francisco during the 1770s. Over the next century and more, periodic earthquakes rocked San Francisco. One quake occurred in 1836, and another rumbled through the area two years later. In 1865 a minor earthquake destroyed part of City Hall and tore up some of the city's water mains and gas pipes. (Powerful earthquakes can destroy

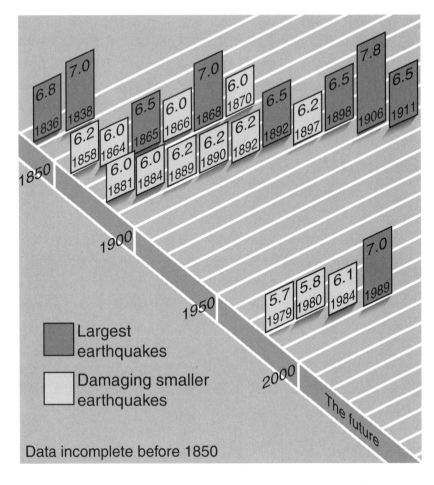

water mains and contaminate major water supplies.) The author Samuel Clemens (Mark Twain), who was living in San Francisco during the quake, described it in his 1872 book *Roughing It:*

> As I turned the corner, around a frame house, there was a great rattle and jar.... Before I could turn...there came a really terrific shock; the ground seemed to roll under me in waves, interrupted by a violent joggling up and down, and there was a heavy grinding noise as of brick houses rubbing together. I fell up against the frame house and hurt my elbow.... I...took out my watch and noted the time of day; at that moment a third and still severer shock came, and as I reeled about on the pavement trying to

keep my footing, I saw a sight! The entire front of a tall four-story brick building…sprung outward like a door and fell sprawling across the street, raising a dust like a great volume of smoke!…

…Dozens of men with necks swathed in napkins, rushed from barber-shops, lathered to the eyes or with one cheek clean shaved and the other still bearing a hairy stubble. Horses broke from stables, and a frightened dog rushed up a short attic ladder and out on to a roof.

A major quake then occurred in 1868, killing five people in the city when they were hit by falling bricks from buildings, as well as 30 others in surrounding areas. Other small earthquakes hit the city in 1890 and again in 1898.

One concern among San Francisco residents was the fires that broke out as a result of the earthquakes. As the quakes rocked houses, stoves were overturned and chimneys collapsed, causing fires to break out and burn down homes. By 1900, the city had about 700 firefighters on duty, located in 80 firehouses in various districts. Nevertheless, a fire department was only as good as the water available to fight a blaze. A report at the time revealed that the city's water system was "inadequate to meet the demands for water flow necessary to fight a conflagration."

South of the main thoroughfare, known as Market Street, were factories and warehouses made primarily of brick that could withstand fires. But many of the small houses where workers lived were made of wood that could easily burn in a blaze. In the Mission District, where the Spanish had built their original mission to convert natives to Christianity in the first days of settlement, many buildings were made of wood. The mansions on Nob Hill were also made of wood, and in the slums of Chinatown, where more than 40,000 people—mostly Chinese immigrants—lived, the streets were packed with wooden apartment houses. Northward, in the sections of Russian Hill, Telegraph Hill, and the Latin Quarter, there were wooden homes and businesses.

Wooden saloons, dance halls, and gambling houses also lined the streets of the infamous Barbary Coast, located along the harbor. One observer called this area of town "the haunt of the low and vile of every kind…thronged with riot-loving rowdies in all stages of intoxication." Indeed, by 1900, San Francisco had become known as "the wickedest city in the world." Some residents of the city believed that the earthquake of 1906 was a form of retribution—a payback—for the sins of the past.

San Francisco Fires and Fire Departments

Fires had been a consistent problem for San Francisco for over half a century before the 1906 earthquake. Devastating fires had repeatedly wracked the city during the 19th century. From 1849 to 1851, several major fires caused enormous damage in the city. The first fire broke out the day before Christmas in 1849. As one reporter wrote: "This morning about six o'clock, the awful cry of fire was raised in the city, and in a few hours property worth more than a million dollars was totally destroyed." An even larger fire broke out in May 1850, resulting in $4 million worth of property damage. The largest fire occurred a year later—beginning in a paint and upholstery store, it was blown by the wind across several blocks of the city. As the strength of the wind increased, the fire roared for 10 hours, destroying as many as 2,000 homes and costing $12 million in damage. As an observer wrote,

> The wind was unusually high, and the flames spread in a broad sheet over the town. All efforts to arrest them were useless; houses were blown up and torn down in attempts to cut off communication [starve the fire]; but the [fire] engines were driven back step by step, while some brave firemen fell victims to their determined opposition.

Despite a well-paid and well-organized fire department, early efforts at firefighting (including on the day of the earthquake) were hampered by the city's inadequate water supply. (Photo courtesy of Charles D. James and Susan Fatemi)

To fight such fires, in about 1850 San Francisco formed a volunteer fire department made up of a variety of volunteer fire companies, such as the Knickerbocker and the Lafayette. As in other cities throughout the United States, volunteers were called out whenever a fire started, but they were often unreliable in their efforts to stop fires. In New York City, for example, fire companies had been known to rush to the scene of a blaze and then brawl with each other for the honor of fighting the fire. Meanwhile, the buildings burned to the ground.

In 1866 San Francisco began a paid fire department and hired a chief fire engineer at a salary of $4,000 annually. In 1893 Dennis

On the day of the 1906 earthquake in San Francisco, this fire engine put out the blazes that raged throughout the Mission District. (Photo courtesy of Bettmann/CORBIS)

Sullivan became chief of the fire department. Five years later, firefighters rushed to the scene of the Baldwin Hotel, a large wooden building that burned to the ground before the firefighters could stop the flames. Chief Sullivan then asked the San Francisco government to add special water mains and build pumping stations that would use salt water from San Francisco Bay to improve the city's firefighting resources. However, such a system would be expensive to develop, and local politicians believed that it was unnecessary, since most fires would not affect the majority of homes and businesses. The city's political leaders refused to build the additional water system, leaving San Francisco without enough resources for the disastrous fires that broke out after the earthquake of 1906.

During that earthquake, as the buildings shook, chimneys were broken and fireplaces belched their flames into the homes of city residents, causing fires. As the earth continued to move, gas mains were wrenched apart, and the heat and flames ignited the hissing gas. The earthquake also broke the city's water lines. Without the proposed water system recommended by Sullivan, San Francisco's fire department was unable to bring water to most of the burning buildings, compounding the destruction that the earthquake caused. Instead, firefighters were forced to use dynamite to level wide swaths of San Francisco, hoping to create firebreaks that would deny the raging flames the fuel they needed to keep spreading. Meanwhile, thousands of residents fled the center of the city, taking ferries across San Francisco Bay to nearby Oakland, California.

After three days, the inferno finally ended as boats were brought in to pump water from San Francisco Bay onto the fires. The scene that confronted the city's residents afterward was almost unimaginable. An area of about 5 square miles (13 km^2), covering a large part of San Francisco, had been devastated. Over 250,000 people had been left homeless—the majority of city residents—while more than 500 had died and thousands of others were injured. As author Jack London, who lived through the terrible disaster, put it, "San Francisco, at the present time, is like the crater of a volcano, around which are camped tens of thousands of refugees."

CHAPTER 2

Disaster Strikes

*A photograph taken
from the top of the
Union Ferry building
in San Francisco shows
the devastated city
after the earthquake
and three days of fire.
(Photo courtesy of
CORBIS)*

As dawn broke over San Francisco on April 18, 1906, the bell from a church tower in Chinatown sounded the hour—5:00 A.M. Pacific Standard Time (PST). Police officer Jesse Cook was walking his beat through the fruit and vegetable markets that were already open for business. Suddenly, he heard a sound coming toward him, ripping along Washington Street. The time was 5:15 A.M. (PST). In the office of the *San Francisco Examiner,* one of the reporters looked out the window and saw buildings "dancing." "It was as if the waves of the ocean were coming towards me," he said, "billowing as they came." The great San Francisco earthquake had begun to engulf the city.

Buildings swayed violently for 40 seconds as the earthquake shook their foundations. The quake stopped, only to begin again about 10 seconds later, and then it stopped again, only to be followed by smaller tremors. (Such smaller tremors are discussed in the "Aftershock" sidebar on page 22.) Thomas Chase, who worked at the Ferry Building, from which passengers took ferryboats across San Francisco Bay, had this account to report.

Power and trolley lines snapped like threads. The ends of the power lines dropped to the pavement not 10 feet [3 m] from where I stood, writhing and hissing like reptiles. Brick and glass showered about me.

Buildings along First Street from Howard to Market crumbled like card houses. One was brick. Not a soul escaped. Clouds of smoke obliterated the scene of destruction. The dust hung low over the rubble in the street.

…As soon as I reached the curb a second shock hit. This was harder than the first. I was thrown flat and the cobblestones danced like corn in a popper. More brick and glass showered down on the sidewalk…. If I had been a block or two further down on First Street I would not be here today.

…When I got to Market Street I noticed the pavement had disappeared…. I went back and around and saw that the pavement had dropped fully five feet [1.5 m]….

The entire south wall of the Ferry Building was out. It crashed through the driveway down into the Bay….

…We went to the office and found the counters and floor covered with plaster. Everything was wet from broken pipes, but water had stopped running as mains had been broken somewhere along the line….

A guest at San Francisco's posh St. Francis Hotel, located near Market Street, recalled,

> I was awakened by a loud rumbling noise which might be compared to the mixed sounds of a strong wind rushing through a forest and the breaking of waves against a cliff. In less time than it takes to tell, a concussion, similar to that caused by the nearby explosion of a huge blast, shook the building to its foundations.

Although the St. Francis Hotel was still standing afterward, other buildings were not saved. Newspaper reporter James Hopper of the *San Francisco Call* later wrote that the rear section of the building where he lived had collapsed. "The mass struck a series of little wooden houses in the alley below," he added. "I saw them crash in like emptied eggs, the bricks passing through the roofs as though through tissue paper." Lloyd Head, only a child when the earthquake struck, wrote years later that he was awakened in his bed as his house shook "backwards, forwards, sidewards...making things dance in the bureau as if they were alive, while the dishes in the pantry and the China closet rattled about at a great rate." Head ran into his parents' bedroom, where he hoped to find safety.

In the southern part of San Francisco, flimsy wooden hotels collapsed, killing some of their residents and creating huge clouds of dust across the area. City Hall, the most impressive building in San Francisco, collapsed when its pillars buckled from the impact of the earthquake. Fred Hewitt, a reporter with the *Examiner*, was near City Hall at the time of the quake. He later wrote,

> It is just possible that the most dramatic point in San Francisco when that terrible rumble began was in the immediate vicinity of that imposing pile, San Francisco City Hall, that structure that cost millions upon millions to erect and years of labor to accomplish.

I was within a stone's throw of that city hall when the hand of an avenging God fell upon San Francisco. The ground rose and fell like an ocean at ebb tide. Then came the crash. Tons upon tons of that mighty pile slid away from the steel framework and destructiveness of that effort was terrific.

In the basement of City Hall was an emergency hospital where patients were trapped by the wreckage. As one policeman reported,

The lights had all gone out. It was black, dark, and smothering. Nobody could see his hand in front of his face, while the scattering bricks and plaster and mortar threw out a suffocating dust that filled wards and corridors and was choking me.... Everybody seemed to be yelling and shrieking at the top of his voice.

The once spectacular City Hall of San Francisco lies in ruins after the earthquake, a demoralizing sign of the disaster. (Photo courtesy of Underwood & Underwood/CORBIS)

Fortunately, none of the patients in the hospital was injured. Rescue workers were able to remove the rubble and transport the patients to a makeshift hospital that had been set up across the street at the Mechanics' Pavilion after the quake had struck. The pavilion was a large theater where variety shows featuring singing and dancing were held. Residents also went to the pavilion to see motion pictures—these were just becoming popular in San Francisco.

Fire Chief Dennis Sullivan was asleep on the third floor of a fire station when he was awakened by the quake. As he walked across the room, smokestacks from a nearby building smashed through the roof and hit the floor. The floor collapsed. Sullivan tumbled downward and was so severely injured that he never recovered.

Even without Sullivan, San Francisco's fire engines were already racing down the streets of the city. Fires had broken out, especially south of Market Street, when stoves and chimneys were turned over as buildings shook and collapsed. The horses pulling one fire engine galloped down Market to a fire raging at a boardinghouse. As historian William Bronson wrote, when the fire company reached the blaze,

> One of the men threaded a hose onto the hydrant across the street and turned the valve. The men who held the hose braced themselves. But there was no rush of water.... They tried the hydrant around the corner ...but the story was the same: nothing but an impotent trickle of muddy water. They tried one more hydrant before the suspicion became a forbidding truth: the mains were broken, and there would be no stopping the fire here.

As fires spread and buildings collapsed, many people escaped to the streets, taking whatever belongings they could carry. One woman carried a birdcage with four kittens inside. A man walked

down the street in his nightshirt until a policeman stopped him. "Say, Mister," the officer said, "I guess you better put on some pants."

When news reporter Hopper left his building and went outside to determine the impact of the quake, he saw hundreds of people walking the streets, stunned by what was happening to them. "The streets were full of people," he wrote, "half-clad...but silent, absolutely silent, as if suddenly they had become speechless idiots.... I saw men and women with gray faces. None spoke." Hopper passed one half-destroyed building where a man was trying to escape from a third-story window by sliding down a homemade rope of cloth. Hopper ran inside to try to help the man, but along the way, he found a woman who had been buried by the debris. He removed the rubble and rescued her from the building. When he went back to help a second woman, he found that this woman was already dead.

Dazed by the disaster, residents of the city flee down Market Street toward the Ferry Building and the bay on the morning of the earthquake. Many carry what few possessions they could salvage from the destruction of their homes. (Photo courtesy of Bettmann/ CORBIS)

Aftershock

About 8:15 A.M. (PST), a major *aftershock*—a weaker earthquake—followed the main shock of the earthquake. The aftershock shook many buildings that had been damaged in the original quake, and they fell to the ground. People began to panic, probably believing that another earthquake was about to occur. "The noise and the dust, and the feeling of destruction, all combined to daze a man," police sergeant Jesse Cook said later. In addition to this aftershock, other, smaller aftershocks followed the earthquake. After a major earthquake, aftershocks can occur for weeks, months, or years.

In another part of the city, Enrico Caruso, considered the most famous opera star in the world at the time, had been jolted out of his bed at the Palace Hotel by the force of the earthquake. In 1875 William Ralston had constructed the magnificent Palace on Nob Hill. The hotel covered 2.5 acres (1 ha) and contained 800 rooms. Caruso had appeared the night before at the Grand Opera House, built in 1876 on Mission Street. On the morning of the earthquake, the Palace swayed back and forth. Caruso was so frightened that he had to be calmed by orchestra conductor Alfred Hertz, who occupied a nearby hotel room.

Hertz asked Caruso if his voice had been affected by the quake. The conductor opened the window in the singer's room; Caruso stood in front of the window and began to sing, his voice as strong as ever. Down below, people running by in their pajamas after being shaken out of bed by the quake stopped to listen to his magnificent voice. No one knew that he was frightened; indeed, one passerby called Caruso's singing "the bravest and best" he had ever heard from Caruso—an "attempt on the singer's part to show the world that at least he had not been scared."

Like Caruso, Peter Bacigalupi was a lover of music. He owned a music store in San Francisco that sold pianos and other musical instruments, as well as phonograph records. After the earthquake struck, Bacigalupi ran downtown, hoping to save his store. He gave this account of what happened after he arrived on the scene:

We...packed all our books [containing the important accounts] in a large basket.... When all this was ready,

I took a trip though the whole store for one last look. You can imagine my feelings on going to the second floor…and seeing every Record standing on its shelf in perfect order.…

After locking all doors…I went to the third floor …[then] the fourth and fifth floors…and then up to the roof. As soon as I got there I saw how hopeless was my chance of saving our building from the fire, which was then burning in front.… The fire was so hot that I decided it was better for us to get away.

…Aside from [the basket containing our books and papers] all we saved was a small hand basket, also containing books. We placed implicit reliance upon a large safe that we had in our office, and which contained all of our valuable books and papers.…

[At a location on Market Street,] I was so overcome with my feelings that I sunk into an office chair, from which I could watch my place on Mission street.… I watched the wholesale house burn; first the roof falling, then floor after floor.

Establishing Authority in the City

During the first hours of the earthquake, the San Francisco authorities tried to take charge of the situation. The U.S. Army maintained two garrisons in the city—one at the Presidio, a military base, and the other at Fort Mason, along San Francisco Bay. The acting commander of these contingents was 40-year-old Brigadier General Frederick Funston. Funston's commander, Major General Adolphus Greely, was not in San Francisco at the time of the quake. (Some highlights of Greely's career are related in the "Adolphus Washington Greely" sidebar on page 24.) Funston had won the Congressional Medal of Honor for bravery during the Spanish-American War in 1898. Three years later, at the young age of 35, Funston had been put in charge of army garrisons in San Francisco and other locations in California.

Realizing that order had to be restored to San Francisco, Funston quickly sent messages to his subordinates in charge of the garrisons at the Presidio and Fort Mason. He ordered them to march their troops into the center of San Francisco to prevent looting and to reassure the residents of the city that order would be maintained. The garrison officers were directed to work with the local police under the direction of Chief Jeremiah Dinan. By 8:00 A.M. (PST), the troops had arrived, and Chief Dinan put

Adolphus Washington Greely

At the time of the 1906 earthquake, General Funston was serving under Major General Adolphus Greely, the commander of the Presidio. Greely had a distinguished career in the U.S. Army. He had fought for the North during the Civil War, being wounded twice. After the war, Greely led a 25 men expedition to the Arctic to establish weather stations. Severe weather forced his team to stay in the Arctic for three years. When a rescue expedition finally reached Greeley, only he and six of his men were still alive. In 1886, Greely published a book about his experiences. The book was titled, *Three Years of Arctic Service: An Account of the Lady Franklin Bay Expedition of 1881–1884 and the Attainment of Farthest North*.

When the earthquake struck, Greely was out of town, on the way to attend his daughter's wedding. When he returned, he assumed command of the army troops. Greely commanded much of the relief effort following the earthquake. The army had a hand in firefighting, law enforcement, sanitation, providing shelter, establishing medical facilities, and distributing food.

them to work keeping order along Market Street. Dinan told them that they were authorized to shoot anyone who was breaking into stores or houses and stealing merchandise or other items.

Meanwhile, the fire department had begun pumping water from the San Francisco sewers to fight the flames that were threatening the city's buildings. Many buildings had been set ablaze by the enormous heat—reaching 2,200°F (1,204°C)—from fires that were already engulfing other structures. Firefighters had hoped to stop the blazes before they struck Market Street. Earlier in the morning, however, a woman living near Market had turned on her stove to make breakfast without realizing that her chimney had collapsed. Instead of going up the chimney, flames from the stove spread fire through the house. This fire—called the "Ham-and-Eggs" fire, because the woman may have been preparing these items for her breakfast—had spread by early afternoon to Market Street. The fire also spread to Chinatown, forcing thousands of residents to flee their homes.

While the fires burned, the mayor of San Francisco, Eugene Schmitz, was heading from his home to City Hall, not realizing that the building had already collapsed. When the mayor learned that City Hall had been destroyed, he went to the San Francisco Hall of Justice. From there, he began to direct operations in the city. Later in the day, the mayor asked 50 of the city's leading citizens to join a Committee of Fifty that would help him run San Francisco during the crisis. Mayor Schmitz issued a proclamation: "The Federal Troops, the members of the Regular Police Force and all special Police Officers have been authorized by me to KILL any and all persons found engaged in Looting or in the Commission of Any Other Crime." Schmitz also decided to strengthen the police force by adding 1,000 volunteers to the department. They were ordered to patrol the streets to prevent any crimes. By the afternoon of April 18, some looters had already been stopped and killed.

Mayor Eugene Schmitz

Eugene Schmitz had spent most of his career in San Francisco as a musician. He was a violinist and an orchestra conductor with a large following in the city. He was especially popular among immigrants in San Francisco, since his mother had been Irish and his father had been German. Schmitz was also a friend of a wealthy and powerful political leader in San Francisco, Abraham Ruef. Having decided to start a new political party in the city, Ruef asked Schmitz to run for mayor in 1901. Although Schmitz had no political experience, he finally agreed after listening to Ruef's persuasive arguments. Ruef told Schmitz, "You have as much experience and

Despite accusations of corruption before the 1906 earthquake, Mayor Eugene Schmitz demonstrated great leadership during the disaster. He traveled throughout the city surveying the damage and offered support to citizens in the aftermath of the disaster. (Photo courtesy of CORBIS)

information as many men who have been nominated and more than some who have filled the office. What you lack can easily be supplied. The speeches and the funds we can take care of."

Schmitz was elected, reelected in 1903, and reelected again in 1905. During this period, Schmitz became rich—he and Ruef forced merchants and other business owners to pay them bribes in order to be allowed to operate in San Francisco. Tavern owners, construction contractors, telephone companies, and cable car operators contributed their share. Schmitz once said, "From boyhood, I had ever heard: Make money, no matter how. People will never ask how you made it, only get it." He was not too concerned whether he made his money dishonestly, because he was convinced that having money was the way to achieve respect from other people.

A group of the city's leading citizens had decided to put a stop to the corruption. They had initiated a probe of Schmitz's operations just before the earthquake hit. Once the earthquake struck, however, Schmitz showed that he was a capable leader during a serious crisis. In fact, he won back the support of many San Francisco residents because of his effective leadership. (Schmitz did eventually face charges of corruption, as detailed in the "Fate of Mayor Schmitz" sidebar on page 59.)

Fires Rage across the City

While Mayor Schmitz and others in authority were trying to keep order, thousands of residents left their homes to find a safe haven away from the fires. Some carried whatever household possessions they could lift, while others loaded some of their valuables into small carts. Many refugees gathered at Union Square on the north side of Market Street. Others made their way down to the wharfs along San Francisco Bay. Boatmen like Tom Crowley, who owned 18 launches, ferried people across the bay to Oakland at a rate of 50 cents per person. Anyone who did not have the money was taken across the bay for free. Ticket clerk Thomas Chase described the crowds who waited to buy ferry tickets on the pier:

> The crowds were gathering fast in the Embarcadero, carrying bundles and suitcases.... They began dropping them on the pavement while waiting to get out. This pile grew until it was like a hay stack....
>
> The people all seemed to be in a daze or stunned. After leaving their bundles they apparently gave no further thought to them. Another lighter shock occurred a little while after 8:00 A.M. [8:14 A.M. (PST)] The crowd surged back away from the Ferry. I closed up quickly and got out into the street. By that time, just a few seconds, it was over.

Eventually, the flames approached the Mechanics' Pavilion, which had been turned into a temporary hospital. During the early afternoon, patients were removed from the pavilion and driven to Golden Gate Park, in the far northern part of the city, near the Presidio. Indeed, the Presidio itself was rapidly becoming a refugee center. But some patients were too close to death to be moved. As one relief worker recalled, "Those with mangled bodies and broken or burned limbs begged to be shot to escape being burned alive. [They] were chloroformed by doctors and nurses and shot by soldiers. It was done as an act of humanity."

In other parts of the city, valiant efforts were under way to save some of the buildings. At the corner of Fifth and Mission Streets was the U.S. Mint, with an estimated $200 million locked away inside its vaults. The mint was a storehouse for government gold and currency. Its superintendent, Frank Leach, had been jolted out of bed that morning when the building where he lived

> danced a lively jig, jumping up and down a good part of a foot [0.3 m] at every jump, at the same time swaying this way and that; the walls and ceilings were twisting

and squirming, as if wrestling to tear themselves asunder or one to throw the other down. Then there were the terrifying noises, the cracking and creaking of timber, the smashing and crashing of falling glass, bric-a-brac, and furniture, and the thumping of falling bricks coursing down the roof sides from the chimney tops....

I lay in bed and saw the debris of wrecked chimney tops go sailing past [the] bedroom windows.... I confess that for a few seconds I was impressed with the idea that the end of the world had been reached.

Once he was convinced that the world had not ended, Leach headed down to the ferry and crossed San Francisco Bay into the city. As he arrived in San Francisco, he saw enormous "clouds of

The U.S. Mint in San Francisco was saved from fire by loyal employees who endured harrowing heat and smoke to keep the flames of surrounding buildings at bay. (Photo courtesy of CORBIS)

black smoke." Leach tried to make his way down Market Street, but there were flames everywhere. Along the way, he passed many people heading to the ferry—where he had earlier landed—to get out of San Francisco.

Leach at last found a roundabout route that was not engulfed by flames and arrived at the U.S. Mint. Across the street from the mint, flames were raging, destroying many small buildings. Inside the mint, Leach found 50 employees, along with some soldiers, working on each floor to save the building.

The heat from the surrounding fires was almost unbearable. Leach later wrote, "The glass in our windows, exposed to this great heat, did not crack and break, but melted down like butter; the sandstone and granite, of which the building was constructed, began to flake off with explosive noises like the firing of artillery." Explosions occurred in surrounding buildings that collapsed in

This picture shows the city of San Francisco engulfed in thick black clouds of smoke as fire swept through the streets, destroying everything in its path. (Photo courtesy of CORBIS)

the fire. "Great tongues of flame flashed into open windows [in the mint] where the glass had been melted out, and threatened to seize upon the woodwork of the interior of the...rooms."

Fortunately, water pipes had recently been laid throughout the mint, with hoses and fire hydrants on every floor. A well, located in a courtyard, supplied water to the building so that it did not have to rely on the water mains throughout the city. Using buckets of water, a pump located in the boiler room, and water from two tanks on the roof, the employees succeeded in dousing much of the building. By 5:00 P.M. (PST), they had saved the mint.

The post office building on the south side of the city was also kept standing, thanks to the efforts of postal workers—but the telegraph office was not so lucky. A telegraph operator had sent out messages throughout the day, providing reports to the rest of the country about the earthquake and the fires. By the afternoon, as the blaze neared the building, the telegraph operator reported, "Fire all around in every direction.... I want to get out of here or be blown up." With that, he left the building just after 2:20 P.M. (PST). Later in the afternoon, flames also reached the Palace Hotel. By this time the guests, including Enrico Caruso, had evacuated the seven-story structure. The hotel was totally destroyed.

The Destruction Continues

Without much water to fight the fires, San Francisco disaster crews began bringing in dynamite to blow up buildings so they would not provide fuel to feed the flames. Dynamiting began in the afternoon, south of Market Street, but it did little to stop the progress of the fires. In some cases, it seemed to set off new fires, which broke out in the wake of the blasts. Nevertheless, there appeared to be no other alternative.

In the early evening of April 18, General Funston met with the Committee of Fifty appointed by Mayor Schmitz. Funston urged

With the fires finally extinguished, San Franciscans began to rebuild their city. One of the first steps was to dynamite remnants of buildings that were still standing but unsafe to occupy or renovate. (Photo courtesy of CORBIS)

the committee and the mayor to let his men begin dynamiting huge sections of San Francisco to prevent the fire from moving any farther north. "There is no water," he said. "The only hope I have of slowing up the advancing fire is by using dynamite. A fire wall can be blasted that will hold the flames until water can be provided." Once the buildings had been blasted, army troops planned to set them alight and start *backfires*—fires that would move in the opposite direction of the main fires and stop them.

Meanwhile, an estimated 100,000 residents of San Francisco had already seen their homes destroyed. Much of the financial section of the city also lay in ruins. The fires had wiped out the huge Crocker Bank and other financial institutions. Before Crocker went up in smoke, bank president William Crocker and his assistants loaded the bank's records into carts and transported them to boats that took them out of San Francisco. Fortunately, the bank's money was kept in huge metal vaults that were not destroyed by the fire. However, the flames left the vaults so hot that they could not be touched for many days, so the bank could not immediately reopen for business at a new location. Other banks suffered the same fate as Crocker. Their buildings burned down, but their records and cash were saved.

San Francisco was not the only community that had been hit by the massive earthquake. In nearby Santa Rosa, buildings had also been toppled by the quake, and those structures that remained were entirely destroyed by fires. In the town of San Jose, south of San Francisco, 8,000 people had lost their homes. But San Francisco had received by far the most damage. Worse would surely follow unless the fires could be stopped.

CHAPTER 3

The Aftermath of the Earthquake

Thousands of refugees relocated to shelters in Golden Gate Park after their homes were destroyed by the earthquake and fires. (Photo courtesy of Bettmann/CORBIS)

Novelist Jack London wrote about his experiences in San Francisco after the earthquake struck the city. His account was published in *Collier's* weekly magazine.

At eight o'clock Wednesday evening I passed through Union Square. It was packed with refugees. Thousands of them had gone to bed on the grass. Government tents had been set up, supper was being cooked, and the refugees were lining up for free meals.

> At half past one in the morning [April 19, the second day of the disaster] three sides of Union Square were in flames.... The fourth side, where stood the great St. Francis Hotel was still holding out. An hour later, ignited from top and sides the Francis was flaming heavenward. Union Square...was deserted. Troops, refugees, and all had retreated.

That was how quickly the fire was spreading.

The firefighters had hoped to hold the flames along Powell Street, which intersected with Market Street just beyond Union Square. Fire engines were fighting the blaze with water drawn from a nearby cistern—a reservoir of water under the ground. By 3:00 A.M. (PST) on April 19, however, the fire had moved across Powell Street and threatened Nob Hill.

On the hill, wealthy business leaders known as the Big Four of San Francisco—Mark Hopkins, Collis P. Huntington, Leland Stanford, and Charles Crocker—had built magnificent mansions during their lives, giving themselves a view of the entire city. After Hopkins's death in 1878, his mansion, with its fancy woodcarvings and a bedroom with ivory and ebony decorations, had been donated to the University of California. The university turned it into an art school known as the Hopkins Institute of Art. Students at the school had worked throughout the preceding day to remove as many paintings as possible before the fires reached the building. "We...played a stream [sprayed water] on the Mark Hopkins Institute and surrounding buildings until the water supply in that cistern under the pavement...was exhausted," explained the captain of one fire station. Then the mansion went up in smoke.

Stanford was the founder of Stanford University, established in 1891 in Palo Alto, California. The grand house he had built had a marble entrance and an imposing hallway to receive guests. But it burned just as fast as Hopkins's mansion. Crocker had helped direct the building of the transcontinental railway that linked the

Nob Hill had been the site of grand mansions built by some of the country's wealthiest business leaders. It was reduced to smoldering ashes in the aftermath of the fires brought on by the earthquake. (Photo courtesy of Charles D. James and Susan Fatemi)

eastern part of the country to the West in 1869, and he later became head of the Southern Pacific Railroad. He had spent $2 million on his home—a huge fortune at the time. The house had a 76-foot (23.2-m) tower on one side and a magnificent collection of paintings. Everything was destroyed in the fire. The last member of the Big Four was Huntington, another railroad magnate, who had established the Central Pacific Railway. The home he had built was also completely gutted by the fires.

Winds then carried the fires to the huge Fairmont Hotel on the side of Nob Hill. The Fairmont was burned to the ground. From Nob Hill, the fires spread across to Telegraph Hill and Russian Hill, nearer San Francisco Bay. The fires raging across the city created a huge cloud of smoke 2 miles (3.2 km) high.

Meanwhile, soldiers were ordering people to evacuate their homes, sometimes before the fires even approached an area. Along Polk Street, some distance from the flames, residents were forced to leave before they could collect any of their belongings.

As one resident said, "The soldiers lacked good sense and judgment...[because] there was abundant time to save many valuable articles which were by this time lost. Why this was done, I did not understand at the time."

The Terrible Inferno

While San Francisco grappled with the fires, help for the city was being organized in other parts of the United States. Congress passed a bill in April 1906 authorizing $1 million for relief aid—later increased to $2.5 million. Trains carrying food supplies began rolling west from New York City; Chicago, Illinois; and Denver, Colorado, as well as northward from Los Angeles, California, and south from Portland, Oregon, and Seattle, Washington. These supplies had been donated to assist the residents of San Francisco, who had no way of feeding themselves.

Meanwhile, Eda Funston, wife of General Funston, was organizing relief efforts at the Presidio. Blankets and food were given to thousands of refugees who were pouring in from across the city. They were also given tents as temporary shelters, while their horses were fed with bales of hay supplied by the army. In one part of San Francisco, the California Bakery was still operating, and bakers worked through the night to make bread that could be distributed to the homeless. The role of the American Red Cross in the relief effort after the earthquake is explained in the "Red Cross and the Quake" sidebar on the following page.

While the fires continued in the central part of San Francisco, flames also spread to the area along the bay. Late in the morning, naval ships arrived from the U.S. Navy Pacific Squadron stationed in San Diego. The ships brought marines and sailors to fight the fires. Along with the naval squadron came two fireboats, the *Active* and the *Leslie*. These ships began to pour water onto buildings along the wharfs that were already being attacked by flames. Engines from the San Francisco Fire Department that pumped

The Red Cross and the Quake

President Theodore Roosevelt ordered the American Red Cross to help in the relief operations in San Francisco. In the past, most cities had depended on their own relief agencies, not a national organization like the Red Cross. Founded in 1881, the American Red Cross had received a new charter in 1905. The director of the Red Cross was Dr. Edward Devine, a professor at Columbia University in New York and author of *The Principles of Relief,* a widely read book describing the most effective measures of bringing relief to areas stricken by disaster. After the earthquake, the Red Cross supplied food and medical supplies for the city's residents.

water from the bay joined the boats. The firefighters kept working throughout the morning until they were almost too tired to lift the hoses. By early afternoon, the fires had died down and almost seemed under control.

Sailors from the *Leslie* also unloaded 500 feet (152 m) of hose that was run into a block of buildings between Nob Hill and Telegraph Hill. According to Lieutenant Frederick Freeman, who filed a report on the rescue efforts,

> This was the only stream of water that ever reached this section of the city; and in feet this was the longest distance that any saltwater stream was taken from the water front....
>
> The stream at this point [would reach] building fronts to a height of about two and a half stories, but when taken to the roofs of four-story buildings, gave sufficient protection to keep the fire from spreading.

Nevertheless, the fires continued advancing through the center of San Francisco, toward another wide thoroughfare, Van Ness

Avenue. Here, the army decided to make a stand, dynamiting mansions along the street and starting backfires by lighting these buildings. The plan also called for dynamiting a large trench in the center of Van Ness, making it too wide and deep for the main fires to cross it. Other facts about dynamite can be found in the "Dynamite and Guncotton" sidebar on the following page.

As the fires drew closer, cars and horse-drawn carts were commandeered to bring in large loads of dynamite from Fort Mason. The army also used artillery to knock down buildings in the area. "I doubt if anyone will ever know the amount of dynamite...used in blowing up buildings," recalled General Funston, "but it must have been tremendous, as there were times when the explosions were so continuous as to resemble a bombardment." Meanwhile,

A dynamite crew stands amid the rubble of buildings that were half-destroyed by the earthquake. (Photo courtesy of CORBIS)

Dynamite and Guncotton

Dynamite was used to blow up buildings after the earthquake in order to create a firewall to stop the advancing flames. This explosive was invented in 1886 by a Swiss chemist named Alfred Nobel. He combined wood pulp with a substance called nitroglycerine to make dynamite. Dynamite was widely used in mining to open up mine shafts, so that coal, silver, and other minerals could be dug out.

In addition to dynamite, the army also used a relatively new substance called *guncotton* to blow up buildings. A French professor named Paul Vieille had invented guncotton in 1885. Guncotton was made from nitrocellulose—a cottonlike substance—mixed with nitric and sulfuric acids. Then it was combined with a gelatin and used like gunpowder to fire artillery shells. However, guncotton was more powerful than gunpowder.

a large squadron of troops was patrolling Van Ness Avenue to prevent looting after the buildings were destroyed. (More about looters is related in the "Looters and Executions" sidebar on page 42.) "Four square miles [10.4 km²] of the city were on fire," Funston said, and "the roar of the conflagration, the crash of falling walls, and the continuous explosions made a pandemonium simply indescribable."

Meanwhile, the winds blowing off San Francisco Bay grew stronger, fanning the fires around Russian Hill and destroying many of the buildings there. The firefighters hoped that the same thing would not happen along Van Ness Avenue. At first, the dynamite and the backfires seemed to be doing their job. Toward evening, however, fires began to creep across one end of Van Ness Avenue. Firefighters rushed to the scene. They climbed onto roofs where the sparks had begun to burn and tore off the shingles to prevent the flames from spreading. By the end of the day, the barrier along Van Ness had prevented the fires from spreading. The neighborhoods behind Van Ness and the refugee centers at Golden Gate Park, the Presidio, and Fort Mason appeared to be safe from the inferno. Thousands of refugees there were spared.

Many people had not waited to see if the fires could be stopped. They were rushing down to San Francisco Bay and boarding the ferries to Oakland. One woman who reluctantly left

Citizens of San Francisco take to the streets to watch the fires burn after the 1906 earthquake. Many people did not wait to see if the fires could be extinguished, but evacuated the city immediately. (Photo courtesy of Associated Press)

Looters and Executions

As the fires spread, looting continued in San Francisco. Soldiers in the army and the state militia—which had been sent into San Francisco by California governor George Pardee—sometimes participated in the thefts themselves. Some soldiers shot civilians who seemed guilty of crimes without waiting to hear any explanations. One refugee was killed at Golden Gate Park after being accused of stealing supplies that she was actually borrowing from her friends.

Mayor Schmitz had ordered that no store owner should make unfair profits during the crisis. Soldiers shot one store owner who was caught overcharging residents for bread. Other people were shot for stealing whiskey from stores. One resident recalled, "I saw five men chained together by a stone wall and a soldier guarding them. I asked this soldier why. He said they were caught robbing the dead and had to be shot at sundown."

Looting is a continuing problem when disasters strike. In 1977 an electrical blackout struck the East Coast of the United States. New York City was plunged into darkness. Looters began to break store windows and steal valuable merchandise. Eventually, the police were successful in controlling the looting.

the city for the ferry dock was Hazel Yardley. Fallen timbers in her home had trapped her two-year-old daughter, Annie. Mrs. Yardley hoped that her daughter might somehow be found alive but believed that the falling debris had killed the girl. Yardley was forced to leave without her. But when Yardley reached a refugee center across the bay in Oakland, the unexpected happened. Mrs. Yardley was reunited with her daughter, who had been saved by rescue workers and was being cared for by Henry and Angela Adams.

In Oakland, 50,000 people were living in makeshift shelters that had been set up in public parks and city churches. Although Oakland had escaped the brunt of the earthquake, Mayor Frank K. Mott warned the people of the city,

> The earthquake…visited upon our city a great calamity, yet it is a source of much satisfaction that we were spared from a conflagration and a serious loss of life.… As many buildings are in an unsafe condition the public are admonished to keep off the streets.… It is also very essential that precaution be used in the building of fires until the chimneys have been inspected and repaired.

Caruso Escapes

Thousands of other refugees left the area by train. Among them was Enrico Caruso, who found a wagon to carry him to the safety of Golden Gate Park. He wanted to leave San Francisco as soon as possible. "You must get me out of here," he said to a servant traveling with him. "I don't care how, but you must do it." Eventually, Caruso convinced a cart driver to take him to the docks so that he could board a ferry across the bay to Oakland. "We pass [sic] terrible scenes on the way," Caruso recalled, "buildings in ruins, and everywhere there seems to be smoke and dust. The driver seems in no hurry, which makes me impatient at times, for I am longing to return to New York." When he saw a line of people waiting to buy ferry tickets, Caruso insisted that he was too important to wait, claiming that he was a friend of the president of the United States, Theodore Roosevelt. At first, the ferry officials did not believe that he was indeed Enrico Caruso—until they asked him to sing. After this, he was permitted to board the ferry ahead of the others. "When we arrive [sic] at Oakland," he added, "we find a train there which is just about to start, and the officials are very polite, take charge of my luggage, and tell me go get on board, which I am very glad to do."

Caruso continued his operatic career, appearing before King Edward VII at Buckingham Palace in London in 1907 and making regular appearances at the Metropolitan Opera in New York City until 1920. But Caruso never returned to San Francisco—he considered it far too dangerous. The devastating earthquake and fires had frightened him, just as they had thousands of other people in San Francisco. Another celebrity's story following the quake is related in the "John Barrymore" sidebar below.

John Barrymore

Actor John Barrymore was the youngest child of a well-known acting family that included his brother Lionel and sister Ethel. The 23-year-old John had come to San Francisco to appear in the role of a drunken telegraph operator in a comedy. Barrymore himself also drank heavily.

Awakened in his hotel room by the earthquake, Barrymore walked into the street on the morning of April 18 and saw the wreckage caused by the disaster. He headed down Van Ness Avenue to Union Square. The square was already filled with refugees. He ran into a friend named William Collier. "What's up, Willie?" Barrymore asked.

"Nothing's up at all," Collier said. "In fact, everything is down. Half the town is burning...."

Barrymore then went searching for a bar that had not been destroyed. He spent much of the next two days drinking and sleeping at the home of a friend.

After the crisis, Barrymore left San Francisco. He later became a star in the movies. He appeared in many films, such as *Grand Hotel, Marie Antoinette,* and *Romeo and Juliet.*

Newspapers Cover the Quake

Although the earthquake brought enormous destruction to San Francisco, the city's newspapers still managed to cover the story. In 1906 San Francisco had several leading newspapers, including the *San Francisco Examiner,* the *Chronicle,* the *Call,* and the *Daily News.* The offices of the first three newspapers were destroyed on the first day of the earthquake. Only the *Daily News* published an edition, running the banner headline, "HUNDREDS DEAD! Fire Follows Earthquake, Laying Downtown Section in Ruins—City Seems Doomed For Lack of Water."

Not to be outdone by the *Daily News,* the editors of the other three newspapers looked around for another location where they could print their publications. Traveling across the bay to Oakland, the editors convinced the *Oakland Tribune* to let them publish from the *Tribune's* office. On April 18, the second day of the disaster, the *Examiner, Chronicle,* and *Call* published a joint edition describing the earthquake and fires.

But newspapers in San Francisco, like those in other major American cities, were very competitive. The *Examiner* eventually pushed out the other papers and signed a separate agreement with the *Tribune* to publish there, while the *Chronicle* made a similar arrangement with the *Oakland Herald.* The *Examiner* was owned by one of the most famous U.S. publishers, multimillionaire William Randolph Hearst. Born in San Francisco in 1863, he had taken over ownership of the newspaper from his father in 1887. Several years later, Hearst had purchased the *New York Morning Journal.* Indeed, he was in New York when the earthquake struck on April 18. After receiving word of the disaster, Hearst dispatched twelve trains with relief supplies to San Francisco. The residents of San Francisco would need these supplies desperately in the days ahead, as they coped with the continuing disaster created in the earthquake's aftermath.

CHAPTER 4

The Catastrophe Continues

A fire engine stands quietly amid smoldering ruins after spending three days in the vicinity of Van Ness Avenue, beating back flames to save the city's Western Addition. (Photo courtesy of Bettmann/CORBIS)

While thousands of people tried to flee San Francisco, firefighters continued to hold the line along Van Ness Avenue to prevent the fire from moving into the city's new Western Addition. In this area were streets lined with thousands of houses. Fire Chief John Dougherty, who refused to give up the fight, led the firefighters battling the flames. Dougherty, a 69-year-old veteran with 28 years as a firefighter, had taken over the department after the

injury to Chief Dennis Sullivan. The struggle against the blaze continued throughout the early morning hours of April 20, the third day of the disaster. With his booming voice, Dougherty drove the firefighters mercilessly. As one observer recalled, "He browbeat the exhausted firemen into an angry fury, until they hated him so much they would rather take a bellyful of smoke and flame than admit to the old man that he could stand the punishment longer than they could."

As the firefighters contained the fire on Van Ness, a violent explosion ripped a large building nearby. The dynamite crews had decided that the building should be destroyed in order to contain the fire. Unfortunately, the building's destruction had the reverse effect, spreading the fire with burning pieces of wood that ignited other structures in the area. The building also contained a warehouse filled with chemicals that blew up, increasing the power of the flames.

As daylight arrived on April 20, the fire was racing up Russian Hill, between Van Ness and San Francisco Bay. The fire was driven by high western winds that were spreading the flames toward the water. While some wooden houses on Russian Hill were saved, many were destroyed. Photographer Arnold Genthe, whose experience is told in the "Arnold Genthe" sidebar on the following page, captured such scenes of destruction across the city on film.

Although soldiers had ordered most people to leave the area, some residents had stayed behind. Using the water that they had stored in their houses, they kept the fires from spreading to their shingled roofs. Volunteers from Russian Hill neighborhoods assisted the residents. The volunteers carried blankets and rugs doused with water. With these, they attacked small house fires wherever they broke out and prevented the flames from destroying some of the homes on top of Russian Hill.

At the same time, another battle was going on to save Saint Mary's Church. Saint Mary's stood near Van Ness Avenue. The huge Catholic cathedral had escaped the fire until late in the

Arnold Genthe

Throughout the crisis, photographer Arnold Genthe took pictures of the devastation caused by the fires. Shortly after the earthquake struck, Genthe grabbed a camera, "stuffed my pockets with films and started out." In one neighborhood he photographed a house that had fallen over onto the street. Its residents had not left, however, and he shot them watching the dark smoke rising from the fires in the distance. Genthe also climbed Nob Hill after it had been gutted by fire. At one mansion, he shot the marble columns in the front, the only things left standing. Another mansion photographed by Genthe had two marble lions in front that had been partially destroyed by the enormous heat from the flames. Genthe also photographed panoramas of the devastation that engulfed the Mission District and other areas of the city. Many of the photos were published in local magazines and books, and Genthe went on to become a famous photographer.

morning of April 20, when flames broke out on the massive church spire. A Catholic priest, Father Charles Ramm, started climbing up the outside of the spire toward the fire. During the first two days of the disaster, Father Ramm had cared for homeless residents fleeing the fire. Now, he was determined not to let the massive church burn. With a cloth bag around his neck, Father Ramm slowly made his way up the tall spire, while pedestrians gathered along the street to watch him. Suddenly, a fire engine arrived, and firefighters erected a huge ladder against the church building. The ladder did not extend far enough to reach Father Ramm. He crept higher and higher, battling strong winds and the heat of surrounding fires. Finally, Father Ramm reached the location where the small fire had started in the church spire. He put out the fire with the cloth bag and then descended the spire to safety.

People in the Russian Hill district look toward San Francisco's downtown, burning after the earthquake. A day later, most of the homes on Russian Hill were destroyed as well. (Photo courtesy of Bettmann/CORBIS)

Destruction Spreads

The full extent of the San Francisco disaster was impossible to ignore. Burial gangs dug graves for bodies of city residents who had been burned to death by the flames. The burial crews also had to deal with rats that emerged from the sewer pipes and ran along city streets through the charred ruins, looking for food.

Bay Street and the elegant mansions of Telegraph Hill lie in ruins after the massive earthquake. (Photo courtesy of CORBIS)

One area of San Francisco that had so far been largely spared was the waterfront. However, the fires gradually moved from Russian Hill, along the Italian neighborhoods of Telegraph Hill, toward the water. Thousands of people found themselves caught in the path of the fire with no place to go. General Funston, from his headquarters in nearby Fort Mason, ordered every boat along San Francisco Bay to head toward the docks. During the afternoon, the boats rescued 20,000 people and brought them to safety. Some residents were not lucky enough to escape the flames, and they were burned to death.

One homeowner, O.D. Baldwin, owned a large brick house near the waterfront and refused to leave it. With the help of his staff of servants, Baldwin used water that he had stored inside his mansion to put out small fires that broke out. Eventually, a team of dynamiters arrived and ordered Baldwin to leave his home because they planned to set a charge and destroy it. Baldwin refused. Since he knew one member of the team, Baldwin finally convinced the dynamiters to leave, and he saved his mansion. The story of another house that survived the fires is told in the "Saving a House" sidebar on the following page.

Meanwhile, the fires from Telegraph Hill approached the docks, where a massive effort began to save the area. The waterfront was an important business area in a leading port city like San Francisco. If it were destroyed, the city would be hard-pressed to restore its financial stability after the fires ended. Navy fireboats stationed in San Francisco Bay poured vast streams of water on the buildings along the waterfront to prevent them from burning. Lieutenant Frederick Freeman, who had already been battling the fires for many hours, directed the relief effort. As one of his men put it: "He looked all in, with the sweat streaking down the grime on his weather-beaten face onto the dirty white handkerchief he had tied around his neck.... I can hear him now, 'Come on, men, sock it to 'em!' And they did." The firefighters were growing increasingly exhausted, as they continued to battle the flames.

Saving a House

A house owned by Eli T. Sheppard survived the San Francisco fire—but just barely. On Thursday morning, April 19, the army urged the Sheppards to leave their home as the fires approached. Although they headed for the ferry to Oakland, a boarder named E.A. Dakin chose to remain in the house. As the fires came closer, Dakin changed his mind and decided to leave. But first he hoisted a large American flag up a pole on the roof. The flag was seen by a group of the 20th Infantry, who rushed to the house and, using water from tubs inside, saved it from the fires.

The firefighters were eventually joined by a contingent of marines, heading back to Fort Mason. The marines began tearing down buildings at the base of Telegraph Hill. If these caught on fire from the flames above, the situation along the waterfront would grow much worse. Unfortunately, the winds increased, making the job of containing the fires more difficult.

Freeman had run hoses from the boats onto the docks to deal with the fire. "I found my hose lines burning," Freeman said, "and had to cut the hose to save any part of it.... At this time it seemed that the whole water front was doomed." Yet the boats in the harbor kept pouring water on the flames, while firefighters on the dock struggled to put out the blaze.

The battle continued during the night of April 20. Chief Dougherty then arrived on the scene. He took a hose from one of the firefighters and began to pour water on the flames himself. This inspired his men to work even harder. As one firefighter tired, a volunteer from the dock area would take his place. Water continued in a steady stream from the fireboats in the harbor. Finally, by Saturday morning, April 21, the fires had been put out.

In other parts of San Francisco, the flames had also stopped burning. Mayor Schmitz inspected the fire teams along Van Ness Avenue and in other parts of the city. "The fire is virtually under control," he said. On Saturday evening, rain began to fall across San Francisco, dousing any small fires that still burned and bringing the crisis to an end. Unfortunately, the rain made life miserable for people who had lost their homes and were forced to live in refugee centers. Frederick Collins, owner of a fashionable women's clothing store, had lived through the disaster. In a letter to relatives, he wrote that

> the rain just poured in torrents, soaking bedding, grass and ground and people's clothes. With it a cold wind. People are draggled with mud, and there is hardly a house left that isn't twisted or unsafe. Some are toppled into the streets. Some are leaning over on their next door neighbors, and stone stairs [have] fallen away from front doors. Church towers of stone have crashed and crushed into homes besides them. Many places crushing the occupants. No one will ever know the hundreds that were killed under fallen buildings and then buried.
>
> …You know what we have lost of course. Our beautiful store, a fifty thousand dollar stock. Everything at our apartments, my library, your paintings and mine …and so on down to just what useful thing we could rush into a valise and to bundles.… Everything else went.

Despite the rain, now that the fires were out, the city could begin the process of recovery. This process would stretch out over the weeks and months ahead.

CHAPTER 5

The Impact of the Earthquake

Without homes or supplies, people set up housekeeping in the street. In this picture, a makeshift kitchen serves the needs of local residents left homeless. (Photo courtesy of Bettmann/CORBIS)

The smoldering ruins of what had been a great city presented a grim picture of destruction. The earthquake and fires devastated 4.7 square miles (12.2 km²), or almost 500 city blocks. About 28,000 buildings had been destroyed—a loss that may have totaled as much as $500 million. More than half the population of San Francisco—at least 250,000 people—was left homeless by the

disaster. At least 500 people had died, while thousands of others had been injured. (Some of this information is summarized in the "Cost of the Quake in San Francisco" sidebar below.) The quake had been the worst disaster in the history of the United States. One observer said that

> one was accustomed to the full-toned voice of a big town, intensified by traffic over the cobbles of Market Street...the strident cries of newsboys, and the clanging of [cable] car bells. All of these are silent; the noises are those of a village; the wagons, express carts, and men on horseback partially screen a ghastly background.

While some of the homeless city residents had escaped to Oakland, most San Franciscans who had not been trapped in the

The Cost of the Quake in San Francisco

The 1906 earthquake was the worst to hit San Francisco in history. None of the previous earthquakes had done nearly as much damage or taken so many lives. Since the 1906 earthquake, no other quake that has hit San Francisco had had such a terrible impact on the city. The statistics related to the 1906 earthquake tell the story.

Duration of crisis	74 hours
Dead	More than 500
Homeless	More than 250,000
Blocks totally destroyed	490
Blocks partly destroyed	32
Buildings destroyed	About 28,000
Monetary loss	As much as $500 million

destruction were living in camps set up in city parks and at the Presidio military garrison. (The fate of one man, trapped for days, is compellingly told in the "Finding Antonio Compania" sidebar below.) To help these stricken residents, $9 million in relief aid began arriving in the city from across the United States. Some of it came from the federal government, which had already appropriated a large package of aid. However, most of the relief came from the charitable contributions of people in other cities who wanted to help the residents of San Francisco.

Trains loaded with food arrived from Los Angeles, Stockton, Sacramento, and other cities in California. More trains came bringing meat, bread, and other provisions from Burlington, Iowa; Buffalo, New York; and Denver, Colorado. In Ogden, Utah, schoolchildren went door to door, collecting donations of bread

Finding Antonio Compania

While many people had found refuge in the tent camps, a search was still under way for those who had been trapped in the destruction caused by the earthquake. Antonio Compania, an employee of a meatpacking company, had walked inside a large meat locker as the earthquake struck and had been locked inside. He had apparently survived by eating the beef hanging inside the locker. The melting ice had also supplied him with some water. But eventually, the water ran out. No one knows what Compania did inside the locker or how he must have struggled to get free—but he could not find a way out. The other employees, who were trying to save themselves, had forgotten about Compania until eight days after the quake struck. They returned with dynamite, blasted away the bricks covering the meat locker, and opened it. Inside the locker, power had not yet been restored. Compania was barely breathing. They brought him outside, where he mumbled a few words before dying from starvation and thirst.

for San Franciscans. The children of a Native American school in Oregon baked more bread for San Francisco. The Barnum and Bailey Circus—an attraction that packed in thousands of people to see its animal acts and trapeze artists—sent $20,000 collected from ticket sales. Almost $500,000 was also collected from people in foreign countries, including Japan, China, France, and England. People in these countries had read about the disaster and wanted to help.

President Theodore Roosevelt decided that the relief efforts in San Francisco should not be left to the city. The "outpouring of the Nation's aid should be entrusted to the Red Cross," the president said. Some historians believe President Roosevelt was concerned that the city's corrupt government, led by Mayor Schmitz, would squander the money coming into San Francisco. (The accusations of corruption eventually faced by Schmitz are detailed in the "Fate of Mayor Schmitz" sidebar on page 59.) At

Shelters were set up on any available, safe land throughout the city of San Francisco. In this picture, City Hall stands in the background behind tents and shacks erected to offer people some sort of protection. (Photo courtesy of Charles D. James and Susan Fatemi)

first, residents of the city were upset, because they wanted to handle their own relief, but Dr. Edward Devine, who led the Red Cross, proved to be a very capable administrator. Devine divided the relief effort with the army. The Red Cross would run the actual relief stations for homeless residents of San Francisco, while the army provided the vehicles and handled the other logistics necessary to deliver all the supplies to the refugee camps. The Red Cross also had to contend with citizens' health problems, as told in the "Outbreak of Diseases" sidebar on page 60.

In the camps themselves, the people of San Francisco were living in a unique situation. In the past, the wealthy residents of the city had built their mansions in exclusive neighborhoods like Nob Hill, while poorer homeowners had been confined to more run-down neighborhoods. Now, rich and poor alike lived together in tents at the refugee camps. Many wealthy people had seen their

A relief station seven blocks long was set up to distribute food to victims of the earthquake. (Photo courtesy of CORBIS)

The Fate of Mayor Schmitz

While San Francisco was cleaning up the debris from the earthquake and fires, several civic leaders believed that the time had also come to rid the city of corrupt politics. Although Mayor Schmitz had been widely praised for his efforts to deal with the disaster, many still considered him a dishonest politician. The U.S. government assigned a special prosecutor, Francis J. Heney, to lead an investigation into Schmitz's dealings. San Francisco businessman Rudolph Spreckels provided financing for the investigation.

By October 1906, indictments had been handed down against Schmitz and his colleague, Abraham Ruef, for corruption. Both men were arrested and brought to trial in 1907. The trial was widely publicized in San Francisco. At first, Ruef claimed that he was innocent but later changed his plea to guilty. He asked the prosecutor to keep him out of prison in return for giving evidence against Schmitz. The mayor was later found guilty and sentenced to five years in prison. He appealed the verdict and was eventually declared not guilty. Ruef, on the other hand, was found guilty of bribery and sent to prison.

homes and all their luxurious possessions completely destroyed by the earthquake and fires. They had little more than the poor whom they had looked down upon from the prominence of Nob Hill. Around the camps, there were 150 relief stations passing out bread, coffee, and other food. All the refugees had to wait their turn to be served—the wealthy just the same as the poor. During the remaining weeks of April and the beginning of May, San Francisco spent almost $750,000 to feed the hungry.

In the tent camps, some families established small barbecues to cook their food. The Red Cross also ran hot food stations,

The Outbreak of Diseases

Health problems were a grave concern for Red Cross officials in the aftermath of the earthquake. In September, an epidemic of typhoid fever broke out in the camps. The city would also suffer 160 cases of bubonic plague. Rats that have been infested with fleas are the carriers of the plague. Plague-ridden rats had been transported from China in ships bringing immigrants to San Francisco's Chinatown. During the late 19th century, some people in San Francisco had been bitten by fleas carrying the plague and died of the terrible disease. When Chinatown burned during the fire that followed the earthquake, the rats escaped from the sewer system and water mains and began running across the city. They tried to get to neighborhoods that were away from the fire, invading garbage cans to look for food. One reporter said of the rats: "Housewives are daily being scared into fits by the flash of a long, gaunt body with gleaming eyes." After the fire, Mayor Schmidt ordered that the rats be exterminated. Approximately 150,000 rats were destroyed.

where those who could afford it were charged 15 cents for a meal, but those without any money were served for free. Some women living in the camps found abandoned sewing machines and pieces of cloth and started to make new clothes to replace those that had been lost in the fires. Still others opened small shops and sold items that had been collected from the rubble.

While San Francisco was trying to feed itself, some residents took advantage of the situation and turned to looting. A man stole food from a Red Cross relief station and made off with it in a wagon. Since most businesses had not reopened, some people used their free time to hunt through the ruins, stealing whatever valuables they could find.

Rebuilding from the Ruins

Many of the homes and buildings in San Francisco had been insured before the fires. Indeed, city residents held an estimated $250 million worth of insurance. They now hoped to collect on these insurance policies to finance the cost of rebuilding San Francisco. Some insurance companies paid their policyholders immediately. Among these were the Aetna Insurance Company and Hartford Fire Insurance Company of Connecticut, the Continental Insurance Company and the Queen Insurance Company of New York, and the California Insurance Company in San Francisco, as well as two British companies. Several German insurance companies, fearful of going bankrupt, refused to pay policyholders. Nevertheless, San Francisco's business owners and homeowners received enough money to begin the massive task of rebuilding.

Meanwhile, the leading banks of San Francisco reopened for business. Many of their deposits were still locked in vaults that were too hot to touch and open, so the banks borrowed money from the U.S. Mint, which had survived the fire. Many of the banks opened makeshift offices in the homes of top executives and began making loans and accepting deposits. At the Bank of Italy, Amadeo Peter Giannini had rescued his deposits during the fire, and he used the money to make loans to small business owners who wanted to reopen their shops. (His story is highlighted in the "Amadeo Peter Giannini" sidebar on the following page.) Some merchants also received help from the Department of Relief and Rehabilitation run by the Red Cross. With financial resources totaling $500,000, the department made loans of approximately $250 each to restaurant and food store owners who wanted to reopen their businesses. This was enough money to get many of them restarted.

The Red Cross also provided other services, such as finding homes for children who had been orphaned when their parents were killed in the disaster. The Department of Relief and

Amadeo Peter Giannini

In 1904 Amadeo Peter Giannini opened the Bank of Italy in San Francisco, initiating financial programs that other banks considered highly unusual. Giannini loaned money to construction workers and small merchants, not just the well-to-do. He also went door to door in immigrant sections of the city, looking for new depositors. When the earthquake began, Giannini headed downtown to his bank. With the help of several employees, he took the bank's money out of the vaults, hid it in vegetable wagons, and brought it to his home. After the fires ended, Giannini's bank was the only one that immediately welcomed new depositors and had money to make loans. Located in an old shed, the Bank of Italy—later, the Bank of America—was considered by San Franciscans to be a "symbol of wisdom, daring and integrity."

Rehabilitation also provided new homes for the aged in San Francisco by renovating the stables at a nearby racetrack and outfitting them with beds, a dining room, a kitchen, and a chapel.

Removing the Rubble

One of the biggest jobs facing San Francisco residents was removing the rubble to clear the way for new buildings. Dynamite was used to knock down the walls that were still left standing in damaged structures. Thousands of workers shoveled the bricks and wood that lay across the city into carts and railroad cars. Where there was no railroad track, new track was laid throughout many parts of San Francisco to speed the removal of debris. The rubble was taken to San Francisco Bay and dumped into the water. New buildings were eventually constructed on the landfill, although they were highly susceptible to severe shaking during another earthquake.

While cleanup efforts were under way across the city, one area still remained a center of controversy: Chinatown. The Chinatown section had been completely destroyed by the fire, and many residents did not want the Chinese back in the center of San Francisco. As the *San Francisco Chronicle* reported on April 27, 1906, "The complete destruction of the Chinese quarter by fire has given rise to a hope that [it] may now be established in some location far removed from the center of town." Some political leaders suggested Hunter's Point along San Francisco Bay. Others wanted the Chinese community moved to an area beyond Telegraph Hill. The Chinese objected to these suggestions. They still owned the property where their homes had been built in the old Chinatown section. Eventually, the Chinese took the matter to court, which restored their original property, and rebuilding began.

Chinatown in San Francisco was destroyed by the 1906 earthquake. Members of the community were forced to wage a legal battle to gain permission to rebuild their homes and businesses on the same sites. (Photo courtesy of CORBIS)

A Positive Twist

Although many people lost their homes in the disaster, builders and construction workers benefited by the damage to San Francisco from the earthquake. By the end of 1906, the number of people employed in these trades had jumped from less than 20,000 to almost 60,000.

Plumbers also benefited from the disaster. The earthquake had broken the water system in San Francisco. After the fires ended, 300 plumbers went to work repairing the water pipes and sewers.

The tent camps throughout the city grew smaller as more and more people moved to other homes. Some 150,000 San Francisco residents had not lost their houses during the fires. Most of the area west of Van Ness Avenue was saved. Some families who had been living in tent camps moved in with residents who had not lost their homes. By the autumn of 1906, the city was erecting small cottages to replace the tents. (The availability of construction and other types of work in the wake of the earthquake is related in the "A Positive Twist" sidebar to the left.) About 6,000 of these two- and three-room homes were built, creating new housing developments throughout the city. Eventually, in 1907, these cottages were taken to the lots that the residents had occupied before the earthquake. As one historian wrote, "Workmen jacked the buildings up off their simple foundations, set them on wheels, and with horses or mules supplying the power, hauled them to the new homesites."

Meanwhile, San Francisco tried to restore city services to its residents. The fate of the telegraph system immediately following the quake is told in the "Keeping the Telegraph Lines Running" sidebar on page 66. Louis Glass, manager of the Pacific States Telephone and Telegraph Company, estimated afterward that the company had suffered $1.8 million in damage to the telephone system. However, the underground cable system had survived the earthquake and fires, even in the areas that had been burned out. As a result, 1,000 telephones were still working in the wake of the disaster, and an additional 4,000 were ready to be put back into service shortly after the fires ended. The telephone company also

installed new switchboards to receive telephone calls and route them to the proper locations. According to Glass, "All our long distance lines were unaffected by the earthquake…and we have handled more long distance telephone business than ever."

The city's gas and electrical system posed a more difficult problem. The gas mains had been broken during the earthquake and gas had seeped out, causing fires and explosions. By the end of April, the San Francisco Gas and Electric Company was preparing to turn on the streetlights in several areas, but there was still much repair work to be done to the gas and electric plants before full service could be restored.

San Franciscans began to rebuild their city almost immediately after the quake. In this picture, Western Union replaces telegraph wires that were destroyed by the fire. (Photo courtesy of Bettmann/CORBIS)

Keeping the Telegraph Lines Running

On April 18, when the earthquake struck San Francisco, the telegraph lines went dead. To find the source of the problem, Harry Jeffs, the telegraph wire chief for the Western Union Telegraph Company, began testing the wires. Jeffs left his home in Oakland and climbed up telegraph poles to test the wires at each point. Eventually, he found the source of the problem, along San Francisco Bay, where a wire had become faulty as a result of the earthquake. After fixing the problem, Jeffs began sending messages to other parts of the state and across the country, giving them the news of the San Francisco earthquake. Western Union eventually set up a new communications center at a small house on the Oakland side of the bay, and by Friday, April 20, the company had 18 telegraph lines humming with messages from its new headquarters.

The Impact on Other Cities

San Francisco may have been the largest community to be damaged by the earthquake, but it was not the only one in California to suffer. Northward in Santa Rosa, the earthquake had knocked down all the buildings in the city center. Seventy-five people had been killed there. The residents of Santa Rosa began to remove the rubble in the aftermath of the quake and immediately started to rebuild. Other towns north of San Francisco that were damaged included Point Reyes, Fort Ross, and Tomales, where two people died. At Fort Bragg, along the California coast, fires swept through the business section, causing serious damage.

Southward, the area around San Jose was heavily damaged by the quake. At Agnews State Insane Asylum, the earthquake destroyed walls and killed over 100 patients and hospital staff. Many of the patients, however, were saved, including one who was discovered alive in the rubble three days after the quake. Fires that broke out in San Jose were put out by the local fire department. Other cities that were struck in the San Francisco Bay Area included Palo Alto and Menlo Park. In Palo Alto, the university established by Leland Stanford suffered serious damage, but as Stanford president David Starr Jordan put it, "It is only an incident in the day's work and does not change the development of the institution in the slightest degree."

Toward a Better Future

Jordan's statement echoed the feelings of many people in the San Francisco area as they contemplated the future. Along Van Ness Avenue, where the fires had been stopped, new businesses opened in the buildings that were still standing. On the city blocks that had been burned out, workers began to erect new office buildings and

New buildings mark the San Francisco skyline just three years after the 1906 earthquake. Some remaining ruins can be seen in the right foreground of the picture. (Photo courtesy of CORBIS)

San Francisco rebuilt itself on an even grander scale after the 1906 earthquake. The Panama-Pacific International Exposition in 1915 showcased ornate exhibition buildings. (Photo courtesy of CORBIS)

homes for city residents. Along the waterfront, many buildings had been saved, and San Francisco continued doing business as one of the world's leading harbors. The Ferry Building had been seriously damaged during the fire. Its restoration began during the summer. As James D. Phelan, a former governor of California and mayor of San Francisco, said, "San Francisco was no ancient city. It was the recent creation of the Pioneers and possessed the accumulated stores of only a couple of generations.... There was, in fine, nothing destroyed that cannot be speedily rebuilt."

By 1910, the homes on Van Ness Avenue and Market Street that had been destroyed during the earthquake and fire had been completely reconstructed. Throughout the city, 25,000 new buildings were erected, many with reinforced concrete to withstand another earthquake when it occurred. Indeed, the entire business section of downtown San Francisco, including the banks, City Hall, and the St. Francis Hotel, was totally rebuilt.

Nine years after the San Francisco earthquake, the city hosted the Panama-Pacific International Exposition, the World's Fair of 1915. Visitors to the fair saw a city that had been rebuilt from the rubble of 1906 and that once again ranked as one of the leading U.S. cities. In its modern stores and office buildings, commerce flourished. San Francisco was one of the ten largest cities in the United States in population. Even after the earthquake, the population continued to grow. From about 340,000 people in 1900, San Francisco had reached almost 500,000 by 1915.

The planning for the 1915 international exposition had begun in 1904, two years before the devastating quake. The plans called for the construction of a small city adjacent to San Francisco. Visitors entering the fair through the main gate walked through magnificent landscaped gardens. The fair's buildings themselves were built partially on the landfill in San Francisco Bay that had been created from the rubble from the fires. Among these buildings were exhibition centers for education, agriculture, food products, and manufacturers, as well as a palace of fine arts with huge paintings by American artists displayed on the walls. Located near the Presidio, the fairgrounds also had a large racetrack, an airfield for planes, and halls where every nation participating in the fair could display its inventions and other products.

People would never forget the earthquake of 1906. Yet despite the devastation, San Francisco had been reborn.

CHAPTER 6

The Legacy of the San Francisco Earthquake

The 1989 earthquake in San Francisco measured 6.9 on the Richter scale. In this picture, a crane has been towed into position to replace a section of the San Francisco-Oakland Bay Bridge that collapsed during the disaster. (Photo courtesy of Associated Press)

Although San Francisco fully recovered from the disaster of 1906, the threat of another major earthquake did not disappear. Along the San Andreas fault, the Pacific plate and the North American plate continue to move slowly in opposite directions by an inch (2.5 cm) or more each year. When these plates lock together, tension builds up until they eventually break apart, resulting in another earthquake.

Predicting Earthquakes

Because earthquakes can cause so much destruction, seismologists have looked for ways of predicting them so that people can move to safety before disaster strikes. Several hours before the San Francisco earthquake of 1906, residents of the city reported that animals seemed more restless than usual. Newspaper reporter James Hopper left his office after finishing his article on Enrico Caruso's performance. Hopper passed a stable on his way home to bed. Suddenly, he heard the whinny of a horse. "I asked a stableman…in the darkened doorway what was the matter," he wrote later. "'Restless tonight! Don't know why!' he answered. And then, with my head poked in, I heard the thunder of a score of hoofs crashing…against the stalls."

Scientists now believe that animals may be more sensitive than humans to small tremors in the earth that may be the first signs of a coming quake. Unfortunately, there may not be enough time to evacuate large numbers of people from an area even if a major earthquake is predicted.

Over the past several decades, scientists have developed sophisticated devices to predict coming quakes. One measuring device, called an *extensometer*, is a rod placed across a fault that records any movement. (Modern extensometers may use tape or lasers.) A similar device called a *tiltmeter* consists of a long pan of water placed across a fault. If the fault moves, it causes movement in the water. Technicians record the movement. With these devices, scientists hope to detect *foreshocks*—small earthquakes that may indicate that a large quake will soon occur. Seismologists also rely on satellites that take pictures of Earth. By comparing pictures taken at different times, scientists can detect movements in the ground. Such movements also produce waves of air that travel into space, where the satellites can measure them.

Unfortunately, no reliable system of earthquake prediction has yet been developed because no two quakes follow identical patterns. Foreshocks, for example, may indicate that a large quake is on the way. They may also reveal that the plates along large faults are gradually reducing the amount of tension built up between them through minor quakes. As a result, a major quake may not occur in the future. There is simply no method that scientists have yet developed to be sure.

One of the methods that scientists use to estimate the probability of a major earthquake is to look at the past history of earthquakes in an area. Based on these studies, researchers believe that there is an 80 to 90 percent probability that a major quake will strike Southern California over the next two decades. There is a 70 percent probability of a major quake hitting the area around San Francisco by 2030.

Safeguarding San Francisco

Since there is a good chance that San Francisco could be struck by another major earthquake, what has the city done to protect itself? After the 1906 quake, San Francisco expanded its water system to deal with destructive fires that might break out if another earthquake occurred. Two large reservoirs were built to supply water to firefighters. Better pumping systems were installed to bring in salt water from San Francisco Bay. The city also built over 100 cisterns that hold small underground reservoirs of water. As a result, San Francisco would not be completely dependent on water mains that could easily be destroyed by an earthquake, just as they were in 1906.

Also as a result of the 1906 earthquake, California gradually began to adopt stricter building codes and better construction methods to prevent structures from collapsing during severe quakes. In 1971, for example, a serious earthquake of magnitude 6.6 occurred in the San Fernando Valley, a suburb of Los Angeles. This earthquake killed 58 people and caused $500 million worth of damage to buildings. Strict building codes, however, prevented

The Transamerica Building stands in downtown San Francisco as a symbol of the modern city thriving in spite of the threat of a future earthquake. (Photo courtesy of Hulton Archives/Getty Images)

many structures from being destroyed. Today, concrete structures in California include steel rods placed in the concrete to provide greater strength for the buildings. Tall structures are also built on flexible foundations that can bend slightly with the movement of an earthquake, instead of cracking. Builders place rubber along with steel between these building and their foundations. They also put shock absorbers in between floors. A computer simulation was used to design the huge, 48-story Transamerica Pyramid in downtown San Francisco so that it could withstand earthquakes. While the top of the building is narrow, the base is much wider—a building design that helped the structure withstand the Loma Prieta earthquake, which struck San Francisco in 1989.

Unfortunately, the Loma Prieta quake indicated that San Francisco still faced serious problems in withstanding the damage caused by quakes. The earthquake, at 7.1 on the Richter scale,

The Marina District of San Francisco was destroyed by the 1989 earthquake that rocked the city. Buildings left in ruins were bulldozed to make way for new structures. (Photo courtesy of Associated Press)

struck on October 17, a day when many people in the area were either at home or at Candlestick Park, watching a World Series baseball game between the Oakland Athletics and the San Francisco Giants. As a result, the business districts in San Francisco were not as heavily populated as usual. Nevertheless, 63 people were killed and almost 4,000 were injured. The San Francisco–Oakland Bay Bridge was shaken, and a piece of the upper deck fell on the deck below, killing one driver. In Oakland, the Cypress Viaduct section of the Nimitz Freeway also collapsed, causing the deaths of 42 people. Many of these motorists were trapped in their cars and crushed by the falling freeway.

Overall, the damage was minimized, because the center of the earthquake ran along a section of the San Andreas fault that was 50 miles (80.4 km) away from San Francisco. Nevertheless, about 1,000 homes collapsed, and $6 billion worth of damage was done in the San Francisco Bay area. Many of the homes, such as those in the famous Marina District of San Francisco, were destroyed because they had been built on water-saturated landfill and mud along San Francisco Bay. The landfill was the same one that had been created there after the 1906 earthquake, where workers had erected the buildings for the 1915 World's Fair. Landfill does not withstand the tremors from a large earthquake very well. Many houses were not sufficiently fastened to their foundations with bolts, and they slipped off during the shaking that accompanied the earthquake. Similarly, the section of highway in Oakland that collapsed had been constructed on soft mud. The region that contained this stretch of highway had also been shaken twice as hard as other areas. Other stretches of the highway did not collapse, because they were built on firm sand and gravel, and because these stretches were not shaken as much by the earthquake.

The possibility of an earthquake in the area had been known for many years. Yet many buildings still had not been properly safeguarded to avoid severe earthquake damage. As author

Thomas C. Hanks put it: "I have spent a lot of time standing the earthquake watch [investigating quakes].... What especially intrigues me about the Loma Prieta experience is why we continue to be surprised by—and suffer from—earthquake effects that really are not all that surprising...."

The 1989 earthquake not only caused death and destruction, but also affected business in San Francisco. Fisherman's Wharf, a popular tourist center, received very few visitors after the quake, because people were afraid to go there. In addition, stores had been destroyed, costing merchants many thousands of dollars in lost revenue.

In 1994 a magnitude-6.7 earthquake hit Northridge in Los Angeles. Fifty-seven people were killed and 12,500 buildings were moderately to severely damaged. Once again, however, strict building codes prevented the destruction of many buildings. In 2001 building codes like those now enforced in San Francisco helped keep damage minimal in a magnitude-6.8 quake that was centered in the Nisqually Flats region of Washington State. This quake shook cities throughout the western part of the state. The quake was almost as powerful as the Loma Prieta quake, but since the Washington quake was very deep, there were few casualties. Nevertheless, some buildings that had not been reinforced and stood on soft soil, including the state capitol building in nearby Olympia, were badly damaged, just like similar buildings in San Francisco.

Some of the problems connected with the San Francisco earthquake in 1906 have been repeated in more recent quakes. In 1999 an earthquake struck a suburb of Athens, Greece. Over 140 people were killed, and thousands of buildings were damaged or destroyed. Like the San Francisco quake, many residents of the suburb stayed outdoors after the initial quake, afraid of aftershocks. Poorly constructed buildings, like those in San Francisco, led to much of the destruction.

An earthquake also struck Izmit, Turkey, in 1999. Although Turkey has regulations about the way buildings should be constructed, they were often not enforced. As a result, over 17,000 people were killed, and thousands of buildings were damaged or destroyed. Aftershocks struck Izmit just as they did in San Francisco.

A quake also struck the Columbian cities of Armenia and Calcara in 1999, killing approximately 2,000 people. Looting was a problem after the quake, just as it was in San Francisco in 1906. The Colombian government had to send 4,000 soldiers to the cities to control the looting.

Preparing for the Future

In 1977 Congress authorized the establishment of the National Earthquake Hazard Reduction Program (NEHRP), designed to lead the effort to safeguard communities from the dangers of severe quakes. Earthquakes strike not only California, but other parts of the United States. Since very few of these earthquakes are severe, it is easy to lose sight of how dangerous a major quake can be. According to one report, a large earthquake in an urban area could result in thousands of deaths and $200 billion of damage. Other alarming statistics about earthquakes can be found in the "Frightening Facts" sidebar on the following page.

Under NEHRP, over the past two decades, engineering research centers have been established throughout the United States to study the safest building methods to be used in areas that could be struck by earthquakes. Other facilities in several states, including California, Colorado, Minnesota, and New York, have been linked together under the Network for Earthquake Engineering Simulation (NEES). These facilities use computer modeling and simulations to study the impact of earthquakes. These studies have led to detailed structural guidelines not only

Frightening Facts

The U.S. National Oceanic and Atmospheric Administration (NOAA) predicts that if an earthquake above magnitude 8 strikes San Francisco, more than 10,000 people will be killed and 40,000 injured. The city is much larger and more populated than it was in 1906, when only about 500 people were killed.

Other parts of the United States, such as the New Madrid, Missouri, area, are also in jeopardy of suffering severe damage from earthquakes. Scientists believe an earthquake of 6.0 or higher at New Madrid is almost certain by 2040. While another earthquake like the one that struck in 1906 is not likely in the San Francisco Bay Area for at least a century, scientists say, smaller quakes can occur much sooner. According to a report by the Earthquake Engineering Institute in 2003, it will take another century to completely safeguard the United States against earthquake hazards at the current level of federal funding.

for new buildings but also for the rehabilitation of existing buildings in order to make them safer.

In addition, seismologists have produced detailed maps of earthquake zones and *active faults*—for example, of the Olympia, Washington, area—and a hazard mapping office has been established in Golden, Colorado. The maps help communities understand the risks from potential earthquakes and develop measures—such as stricter building codes—to reduce the impact of quakes. Nevertheless, NEHRP has recently reported that some communities have chosen to disregard this information and develop new neighborhoods in areas that could easily be struck by a severe earthquake. In addition, these communities have not followed the proper guidelines in constructing new buildings or improving existing structures.

According to a 2003 study by NEHRP, at least 75 million Americans in 39 states live with the risk of a major earthquake. Since a major quake is an unusual occurrence, it is easy to ignore the risks. In 1906 the people of San Francisco were unaware that they lived in jeopardy of a severe earthquake. Only after the quake struck did they become fully aware of the danger. Since that time, scientists have learned far more about the causes and the locations of earthquakes. Since quakes cannot be predicted, the only alternative is to institute the necessary safeguards, such as strict building codes, to prevent the damage and loss of life that could result from a repeat of 1906.

CHAPTER 7

Conclusion

The thriving city of San Francisco remains vulnerable to future sizable earthquakes that will inevitably lead to property damage and loss of life. (Photo courtesy of Associated Press)

An earthquake is one of the world's most destructive natural disasters. Certainly, the San Francisco earthquake of 1906 demonstrated the enormous power of a major quake in laying waste to one of the greatest U.S. cities. The impact of the earthquake was even greater than it might have been because San Francisco was unprepared. Its political leaders ignored the advice of Fire Chief Dennis Sullivan to provide better water resources that were independent of the city's water mains. As a result, after the earthquake

struck and the mains were broken, San Francisco lacked the water delivery system necessary to fight the fires that broke out across the city. Firefighters had to fall back on dynamiting to create backfires. But dynamite proved to be an ineffective tool—and in some cases even caused more fires—except at Van Ness Avenue, where the San Francisco Fire Department finally made a successful stand and stopped the spread of the blaze.

Nevertheless, the heroic actions of the firefighters, the U.S. Army, and private citizens showed the courage and stamina of people to deal with disaster and to recover. By 1915, San Francisco had completely rebuilt itself and hosted the World's Fair.

The threat of a major earthquake, however, has not passed. A quake could strike San Francisco at almost any time. To help detect further earthquakes, scientists in California planned to place a probe deep inside the San Andreas fault. Called the San Andreas Fault Observatory at Depth (SAFOD), it would be lowered into a hole bored in Earth's crust. Drilling of the hole to a depth of 2.4 miles (3.9 km) began in June 2004. With sensitive instruments inside SAFOD, scientists hope to study the temperature of the earth and how far the rocks are moving along the fault. Another part of the project calls for placing a series of seismometers in the area. They will take pictures of Earth's crust that can be studied when small quakes occur. With all of this information, scientists hope to detect movements of the San Andreas fault that may predict another major quake.

Drilling the hole for SAFOD was not an easy job. Scientists expect the process to take about three years. Then the hole must be protected with cement to safeguard the observatory. The National Science Foundation (NSF) EarthScope Project sponsors SAFOD.

At present, a quake still cannot be prevented or predicted. In this respect, it is not like a hurricane, which weather forecasters can see forming in the Caribbean Sea. Forecasters can then predict the path of the storm with relative accuracy and warn people to evacuate before the hurricane strikes. Since earthquakes do not give this type of warning, the only alternative is for residents who live in a quake zone to be prepared. This means taking full advantage of all the knowledge developed since the last major earthquake to build stronger structures.

In many parts of the world, laws have been passed to use safer building methods, but the laws have not been enforced. A recent report on the earthquake that struck Izmit, Turkey, in August 1999 stated that "much of the devastation was due to profiteering contractors who ignored earthquake building codes in order to save money." Contractors must also avoid construction in areas especially prone to earthquake damage. In addition, communities need to keep all firefighting, rescue, and medical resources in a condition of constant preparedness. These are the only ways to reduce the impact of another natural disaster like the great San Francisco earthquake of 1906.

Time Line

1906

April 18, 5:15 A.M. (PST)	The earthquake strikes San Francisco; buildings topple over and fires break out
April 18, 8:00 A.M. (PST)	Army troops occupy the center of San Francisco; they begin the task of keeping order and dealing with the effects of the earthquake
April 18, 8:15 A.M. (PST)	An aftershock occurs that creates panic among many residents of San Francisco
April 18, 10:30 A.M. (PST)	The "Ham-and-Eggs" fire breaks out and begins to spread to other buildings in San Francisco
April 18, 12:00 P.M. (PST)	Evacuation begins at Mechanics' Pavilion as fire spreads to the building
April 18, 3:00 P.M. (PST)	Mayor Schmitz appoints the Committee of Fifty to oversee the work of lessening the impact of the earthquake
April 18, 6:30 P.M. (PST)	The Palace Hotel, one of the city's most magnificent buildings, is destroyed by fire
April 18, 9:00 P.M. (PST)	Workers save the U.S. Mint after a seven-hour battle with fires
April 18, evening	General Funston urges massive use of dynamite to stop the fires; water is unavailable due to broken water mains
April 19, 2:30 A.M. (PST)	The St. Francis Hotel, a San Francisco landmark, catches fire and burns

Photo courtesy of Charles D. James and Susan Fatemi

*Photo courtesy of
Charles D. James
and Susan Fatemi*

*Photo courtesy of
Charles D. James
and Susan Fatemi*

April 19, early morning	The fires gut the mansions on Nob Hill that had been built by wealthy San Francisco businessmen during the late 19th century
April 19, 10:00 A.M. (PST)	The Fairmont Hotel is destroyed by fire after its guests have already evacuated the building
April 19, morning	The U.S. Navy Pacific Squadron unloads marines and sailors to fight the fires; fireboats spray water along the docks to save the waterfront
April 19, 6:00 P.M. (PST)	Firefighters start to dynamite mansions on Van Ness Avenue to stop the fires
April 19, evening	The fires reach Van Ness Avenue and begin to burn the buildings along the street
April 20, 5:00 A.M. (PST)	Firefighters battle flames along Van Ness Avenue so they will not spread to a wider area
April 20, 9:00 A.M. (PST)	The blazes begin to reach homes on Russian Hill and Telegraph Hill
April 20, 12:00 P.M. (PST)	Father Charles Ramm climbs up the steeple on Saint Mary's Church and puts out the fire that threatens to destroy the building
April 20, afternoon	The fires spread along the waterfront; many residents are evacuated
April 20, early evening	Navy ships and firefighters battle the fire on the docks until early the following morning
April 21, 7:15 A.M. (PST)	The fires end after a three-day battle by the firefighters, soldiers, and sailors who tried to contain them
April 21, 8:00 P.M. (PST)	Rains arrive; the smoke from charred buildings smolders across San Francisco

Late April   Workers begin to remove rubble from city while plans are made to rebuild

May   Telephone service is restored, enabling San Francisco residents to communicate with the outside world

Late spring and summer   Electricity and gas lines are slowly repaired, and 6,000 new homes are built for homeless San Francisco residents

Photo courtesy of Charles D. James and Susan Fatemi

1906–1910

The homes on Market Street and Van Ness Avenue are rebuilt; San Francisco's financial center is restored; a new Palace Hotel is built; the St. Francis Hotel is reconstructed

1915

February–December   After completely rebuilding, San Francisco hosts the World's Fair

Chronology of Earthquakes

The following list is a selection of major earthquakes of the last 100 years.

1905

April 4

Kangra, India

Magnitude 8.6

19,000 killed

1906

April 18

San Francisco, California,
    United States

Magnitude 8.3

503 killed

August 16

Valparaiso, Chile

Magnitude 8.2

20,000 killed

1908

December 28

Messina, Italy

Magnitude 7.2

70,000–100,000 killed

1915

January 13

Avezzano, Italy

Magnitude 7.5

29,980 killed

1920

December 16

Gansu, China

Magnitude 8.6

200,000 killed

Photo courtesy of Charles D. James and Susan Fatemi

1923

September 1

Outside of Tokyo, Japan

Magnitude 7.9

143,000 killed

1927

May 22

Nan-Shan, China

Magnitude 7.9

200,000 killed

1932

December 25

Gansu, China

Magnitude 7.6

70,000 killed

1935

May 30

Quetta, India

Magnitude 7.5

50,000 killed

1939

January 25

Chillan, Chile

Magnitude 8.3

28,000 killed

December 26

Erzincan, Turkey

Magnitude 7.8

30,000 killed

1950

August 15

Assam, India

Magnitude 8.6

1,530 killed

1960

February 29

Agadir, Morocco

Magnitude 5.7

12,000 killed

May 21–30

Chile

Magnitude 9.5

5,700 killed

Photo courtesy of Charles D. James and Susan Fatemi

1962

September 1

Northwest Iran

Magnitude 7.3

12,230 killed

1968

August 31

Northeast Iran

Magnitude 7.3

12,000 killed

1970

May 31

Northern Peru

Magnitude 7.9

66,000 killed

1971

February 9

San Fernando, California,
   United States

Magnitude 6.6

58 killed

1976

July 27

Tangshan, China

Magnitude 7.5

255,000 killed

1985

September 19

Michoacan, Mexico

Magnitude 8.0

9,500 killed

1988

December 7

Soviet Armenia

Magnitude 6.8

55,000 killed

1989

October 17

Santa Cruz County, California,
   United States

Magnitude 7.1

63 killed

Photo courtesy of Charles D. James and Susan Fatemi

1990

June 21

Northwestern Iran

Magnitude 7.7

50,000 killed

1994

January 17

Northridge, California,
United States

Magnitude 6.7

57 killed

1999

January 25

Northwestern Colombia

Magnitude 6.2

More than 2,000 killed

August 17

Izmit, Turkey

Magnitude 7.6

More than 17,000 killed

September 7

Athens, Greece

Magnitude 6.0

143 killed

2001

January 26

Gujarat, India

Magnitude 7.7

20,000 killed

February 28

Nisqually, Washington,
United States

Magnitude 6.8

None killed

2003

December 26

Bam, Iran

Magnitude 6.6

30,000 killed

2004

December 26

Indian Ocean

Magnitude 9.0

More than 44,000 killed

Photo courtesy of Charles D. James and Susan Fatemi

Glossary

active fault　A fault where activity has occurred in the recent past

aftershock　A minor shock that comes after the main shock of an earthquake

backfires　Small fires set to stop the advance of a large fire

body wave　An underground wave produced by an earthquake

epicenter　The point on the surface of Earth above the focus of an earthquake

extensometer　An instrument for measuring extremely small measures of expansion or contraction; used to record movement along a fault

fault　A crack that opens where crustal plates come together or within a plate

focus　Another term for hypocenter

foreshock　A small shock that occurs before an earthquake

hypocenter　The point where an earthquake originates beneath Earth's surface.

Mercalli scale　A scale that measures the strength of an earthquake by the amount of destruction that it causes

moment magnitude scale　A scale that measures the strength of an earthquake by the amount of total energy that it releases; it is more precise than the Richter scale

plates   Large sections of Earth's crust that are in constant, slow motion

plate tectonics   A theory that states that Earth's crust consists of large plates in motion

primary wave   A type of rapidly moving body wave that travels from the center of an earthquake through rocks in Earth

Richter scale   A scale that measures the strength of an earthquake by the amount of energy that it releases

San Andreas fault   A large fault that runs along the floor of the Pacific Ocean and along western California

secondary wave   A type of body wave that moves more slowly than primary waves

seismic wave   An energy wave sent out by an earthquake

seismogram   A graph of an earthquake created by a seismograph

seismograph   A device that records energy waves from an earthquake

seismologist   A scientist who studies earthquakes

tiltmeter   An instrument for measuring angles of slope or inclination; used to record movement along a fault

tsunami   Japanese for "harbor wave"; a great wave resulting from shock waves created by an earthquake

Further Reading and Web Sites

Allen, Missy, and Michel Peissel. *Dangerous Natural Phenomena.* New York: Chelsea House, 1995. This book presents a clear, easy-to-read description of natural disasters such as earthquakes.

American Red Cross—History Timeline. On this web site, the Red Cross describes its role in various disasters, which are presented chronologically from the 19th century. Available online. URL: http://www.redcross.org/museum/briefarc.html. Accessed March 30, 2004.

The Association of Bay Area Governments (ABAG) Earthquake Info—Kids Zone. This web site explains important information about earthquakes for students. Available online. URL: http://www.abag.ca.gov/bayarea/eqmaps/kids.html. Accessed March 30, 2004.

Bolt, Bruce A. *Earthquakes.* New York: W.H. Freeman Company, 2003. An introduction to earthquakes, including measurement, effects, and a discussion of plate tectonics.

British Broadcasting Corporation (BBC) News—Deadly History of Earthquakes. On this site students can see a chronological list of the worst earthquakes of the 20th and 21st centuries. Available online. URL: http://news.bbc.co.uk/1/hi/world/2059330.stm. Accessed April 1, 2004.

Bronson, William. *The Earth Shook, The Sky Burned.* Garden City, N.Y.: Doubleday, 1959. This picture book of the 1906 San Francisco earthquake has over 400 photographs.

Chippendale, Lisa. *The San Francisco Earthquake of 1906.* Philadelphia: Chelsea House, 2001. The author presents a timely account, complete with all the latest information, about the great earthquake.

Davis, Lee. *Natural Disasters.* Revised Edition. New York: Facts On File, Inc. 2002. This book contains facts and figures about natural disasters around the world, including earthquakes.

Erickson, Jon. *Quakes, Eruptions, and Other Geologic Cataclysms.* New York: Facts On File, 2001. This book presents complete scientific information about the causes of earthquakes, volcanic eruptions, and other natural disasters.

The Exploratorium—The Great Shake: San Francisco, 1906.The web site of this San Francisco museum has an online exhibit detailing the 1906 quake. Available online. URL: http://www.exploratorium.edu/faultline/1906/. Accessed November 13, 2004.

EyeWitness to History.com—The San Francisco Earthquake, 1906. On this web site, students can find accurate information about the earthquake of 1906. Available online. URL: http://www.eyewitnesstohistory.com/sfeq.htm. Accessed March 30, 2004.

Hetsch, J.E. *San Francisco Earthquake and Fire, 1906: Observations, Criticisms, Comparisons and Opinions on Fire Prevention.* San Francisco: J.E. Hetsch 1907. This was the first book printed after the earthquake and provides an interesting contemporary account of the disaster.

The January 17, 1994, Northridge, California, Earthquake—An EQE Summary Report, March 1994. This web site explains the causes of the 1994 earthquake and its impact. Available online. URL: http://www.eqe.com/publications/ northridge/executiv.htm. Accessed March 30, 2004.

Jeffers, Paul. *Disaster by the Bay: The Great San Francisco Earthquake and Fire of 1906.* Guilford, Conn.: Lyons Press, 2003. This is one of the best modern books to present a complete description of the 1906 earthquake.

Kurzman, Dan. *Disaster! The Great San Francisco Earthquake and Fire of 1906.* New York: HarperCollins, 2001. This book provides many contemporary accounts of the earthquake. Includes a time line that runs throughout the narrative.

Levine, Ellen. *If You Lived at the Time of the Great San Francisco Earthquake.* New York: Scholastic, 1992. This book describes the experience of living through the great earthquake.

National Park Service, U.S. Department of the Interior, Golden Gate Recreation Area; Presidio of San Francisco— Firefighting and Dynamiting, 1906 Earthquake. This web site explains the role of firefighters and dynamiting parties of soldiers in the wake of the 1906 earthquake. Available online. URL: http://www.nps.gov/prsf/history/1906eq/firedyn.htm. Accessed March 30, 2004.

ReadinessInfo.com—All About Earthquakes! How Earthquakes Happen. This web site clearly explains how earthquakes occur. Available online. URL: http://www.readinessinfo.com/eqgeology.shtml. Accessed March 30, 2004.

Schulz, Sandra S., and Robert E. Wallace. U.S. Geological Survey (USGS) General Interest Publication (GIP): "The San Andreas Fault." At this web site, readers will learn all about the great California fault. Available online. URL: http://pubs.usgs.gov/gip/earthq3/. Accessed March 30, 2004.

Sea-River Newsletters—Tsunamis: Causes and Effects. This web site describes the tsunamis—the enormous waves—that often accompany earthquakes. Available online. URL: http://sea-river.com/126_1_gb.php. Accessed March 30, 2004.

Sherrow, Victoria. *San Francisco Earthquake, 1989: Death and Destruction.* Berkeley Heights, N.J.: Enslow, 1998. This is a book for a young adult audience that discusses the causes and impact of the 1989 earthquake.

Stein, R. Conrad. *The Story of the San Francisco Earthquake.* Chicago: Children's Press, 1983. This book vividly describes the catastrophic 1906 earthquake and resulting fires that destroyed much of the city of San Francisco.

Thomas, Gordon, and Max Morgan Witts. *The San Francisco Earthquake.* New York: Stein and Day, 1971. This is probably the best and most complete book on the 1906 earthquake.

United States Geological Survey (USGS) Earthquake Hazards Program—Earthquakes for Kids. This web site lists the largest earthquakes to occur in the United States. Available online. URL: http://earthquake.usgs.gov/4kids/. Accessed March 30, 2004.

The Virtual Museum of the City of San Francisco—The Great 1906 Earthquake and Fire. This is the best web site on the 1906 earthquake. Provides many eyewitness accounts and discusses the role of the San Francisco Fire Department and the U.S. Navy in the aftermath of the quake. Available online. URL: http://www.sfmuseum.org/1906/06.html. Accessed March 30, 2004.

The Virtual Times: The Great New Madrid Earthquake. On this web site, readers can learn about the earthquakes that occurred around New Madrid, Missouri, early in the 19th century. Available online. URL: http://hsv.com/genlintr/newmadrd/index.htm. Accessed March 30, 2004.

Index